The
Silent
Speaker

An Open Letter to My Daughters

Megan Ross

ISBN 979-8-89345-511-3 (paperback)
ISBN 979-8-89345-512-0 (digital)

Christian Faith Publishing
832 Park Avenue
Meadville, PA 16335
www.christianfaithpublishing.com

Printed in the United States of America

The Silent Speaker

Who or what is that little voice that lives deep within us that speaks to us, the voice we all have that can shape our future and our life? Who controls the voice that tells us we are amazing, made to perfection, and can do anything we put our mind to? Who controls the voice that tells us we will never get ahead, we will never be pretty or thin enough or get out of addiction, anxiety, or depression? What controls that inner voice? Who can combat that voice when it goes into darkness? Who or what gives us the power to stand up and fight against it? I sit here and have all these questions running through my mind. As a parent and raising two young daughters, I needed answers. I wanted answers as I see so much darkness in our world right now, answers for myself so I could educate and teach my kids how to be aware and fight that inner voice if it ever goes into darkness. People may often think we would be aware or know if a friend, family member, or their own child is suffering or struggling with life. We would somehow see a sign, but that's not always the case. I've had a number of friends who were thriving and living their best life who ended up taking it. It's silent, shows no struggle on the outside but wreaks havoc on the inside. Why is suicide so prevalent right now and taking so many precious souls? The only clear solution for me was to take a deep dive into my own life, my experiences, to peel back the layers. Go through the highs and the lows to see if there was a connection between my inner voice (the one no one can see or hear, only me) versus the outer voice (the voice of the flesh being influenced by our society, the one the world sees). Is there a connection between the two and who is controlling them, ourselves, or a higher being not of this world? That's where my journey begins.

Finally, be strong in the Lord and in the strength of his might. Put on the whole armor of God, that you may be able to stand against the wiles of the devil. For we are not contending against flesh and blood, but against the principalities, against the powers, against the world rulers of this present darkness, against the spiritual hosts of wickedness in the heavenly places. Therefore take the whole armor of God, that you may be able to withstand in the evil day, and having done all, to stand. (Ephesians 6:10–13)

To my daughters,

You're too young to read or understand this now, but in a way, your life is perfect. You have a mom and dad who loves you more than life itself. You have a huge family that will always love you and accept you for who you are. You don't ever have to pretend to be someone you aren't. I probably have shielded you from the evils of the world up to this point. One day I will have to let you go. One day you'll be an adult, experiencing life on your own, and making decisions for yourself. I am writing this so you have something to read and fall back on if you ever find yourself lost, looking for answers, dealing with depression or anxiety, or going through a hard time. I want you both to be aware of what you could experience when you're old enough to join the various social media platforms. I want you to understand why I said no every time you asked to have a YouTube channel or TikTok account. I want you both to be able to handle whatever life throws at you. I want to share a time in my life that completely changed me and my outlook on life. I want to share a time in my life God saved me.

Growing up, you probably thought Mommy was invincible, knew how to handle every situation. Mommy was there to put Band-Aids on all your scrapes and bruises, help with homework, be your chauffer, and cheer you on at every sporting or cheer event. You were and are my priority. That's the joys of childhood. You only see Mommy doing everything she can to be the best parent for you. It may seem like I had it all together, but in reality, that couldn't have been farther from the truth. I went through a time in my life where I was living for myself but trying to be perfect in the process. I got caught up living how our society teaches us to live that I forgot what was important. I became selfish and spent many nights distracted by things that didn't matter. I got lost along the way but eventually found my way back. I want you to know that as you get older, it's okay if you get lost. It's okay if you don't have it all together. Knowing who to turn to and live for is my purpose for you and the reason I am writing this book. Knowing who to turn to in times of trial could mean the difference between life and death. I want you two to grow up knowing what true happiness looks and feels like. I want you to grow up knowing what true love feels like, not from a boyfriend but from within yourself, a love that only God can give you. I want you to enjoy life and kick ass along the way. I want you to find the strength to live out your purpose and to stand up for what you believe in. I want you to learn when to hold your tongue (that one is a hard one for your mom) and walk away. I want you to learn how to pray and to learn the importance of helping others. I want you to learn to repent and forgive yourself for your sins. We're all sinners, so learning to forgive oneself and one another is crucial.

As you become adults, I want you to know it's okay to make mistakes. Mistakes are actually a good thing; that's how we learn. It's okay to not know your purpose right away. I'm thirty-nine and just starting to understand mine. It's also okay to be different. If everyone were the same, life would be boring. Picking your inner group is important.

We live in a broken world, and keeping friends close that encourage and walk with you in faith is important. Always be nice, and show everyone love and compassion, whether you agree with them or not. Everyone battles their own evil that lives within them; love them through it. Treat everyone with kindness because you never know what pain people are living with or what spiritual battle they are fighting.

What you're about to read will give you a little insight into what I experienced while blogging. I want you to know, social media isn't all bad, but learning to protect your mind is crucial. Don't let it control your life. Always be able to sit with your feelings and meditate in quiet. Letting your brain rest will keep you focused and helps reduce anxiety. When you're old enough, be aware of how long you scroll through different feeds and how you feel when you log off. Who you choose to follow on these platforms matters the most. If you follow the wrong people, it can leave you feeling less than or feeling that your life doesn't look as glamorous as someone else's. Comparison will rob you of your happiness. That's why it's so important to take breaks from different apps. Don't worry; the world won't forget about you. You will still be relevant. It's healthy to be present in your own life and not some virtual reality, and it's so important to read Scripture. It's the only way to battle evil that lives in our world while remaining happy walking through it. If you're too busy scrolling through different people's lives, you may miss the life and the purpose God has for you. I almost did. I can say, without a shadow of a doubt, it's never too late to ask God for help and allow Him to work in your life. You may have people who question your beliefs or look down on you because you live your life differently. That's okay. The people who are supposed to be in your life will be there and rooting for you along the way. It's hard for me to explain in words, but when you allow God to lead your life, you will develop a deep intuition that lives inside you. It makes you look at the world and people differently. It's unexplainable, but there will be a calmness and peace that comes along with it. The more you read and understand the Bible, the more you will stay connected to God and learn how to trust and have faith in things you can't see or understand. I've found His plan always works for the greater good. The last thing I want you to remember is to never give up. When times get hard, and they will at some point, never give up on yourself or your beliefs. Just remember, sometimes we go through situations that seem unfair or bring extreme sadness, but God will let us go through them to help stir up the fight and passion He put within us. I'm not meaning a physical fight but a fight to help people find Christ and battle the evil that lives within this world. When you personally experience what He can do for your life, it will make going through the rough patch a little easier until you reach your blessing at the end. One last thing, don't forget to thank Him. Thank Him for the good and the bad days because you are still breathing on this earth.

I'll love you forever. I'll like you for always. As long as I'm living, my baby you'll be *(written by Robert Munsch)*.

Love you,
Mom

Prologue

A few years ago, I had a strong feeling I should be doing something different in my life. I felt like I wasn't where I needed to be. Something was missing, but I had no clue what it was. I imagine a lot of people at some point in their life have experienced this feeling. My next thought was to start thinking about what *I* love to do, what *my* interests are, what would make *me* happy, and what would make *me* the most money. Obviously, my thought process back then was clearly only about me, not *Him*. To be honest, it never crossed my mind until later, years later, when He saved me. As I begin to share my experience, you'll learn I started a fashion and beauty blog. I was experiencing life on social media, something that was new because I didn't grow up with technology. Other than a flip phone, I didn't have Internet on my actual phone until well after college. I went into the blogging experience, thinking how fun it would be to get paid to shop and live out my passion, styling myself and other people. How glamorous it would be. Becoming a fashion and beauty blogger must be what I was supposed to be doing at this stage of life. So I took a chance and started blogging. I was having the time of my life, so I thought. Don't get me wrong; there are some really amazing things that come with being on social media and blogging, but there is a dark side too. I didn't realize the dark side until I stopped and looked at it through a different lens. From that different perspective, I found myself wanting to not only warn my daughters but also other parents of young adults with what the side effects or red flags of social media really are. I felt God putting it on my heart, at three in the morning if we're being exact, to share in a book what I went through. Thinking about putting my own experience out there for the world to see made me feel scared and vulnerable. I prayed and prayed about it. I remember saying to God one night in my prayers, after having this overwhelming feeling to write this book, "Are You sure? You do know who You're talking to. Me? I've never written a book in my life other than a paragraph or two for my blog."

Short and sweet was my motto for writing, and that would hardly qualify me for being an author of a book. I thought of all the what ifs. My life would change, but would it change for the better? Every day I would wake up and have this same overwhelming feeling to write this book. I was scared of what people would think. I was scared I would lose friends. I was scared I wasn't adequate enough to write a book. I was scared to tell my story. Something kept me scared until God took over. It finally hit me while praying one day. I was ignoring this feeling because of what I thought my limitations are and what people would think. I was ignoring my purpose. Maybe this was His plan all along to help me realize that I am strong through my faith, and I can help others achieve the same awakening. It completely changed my view on God the Father, Jesus, and the

Holy Spirit. Being on social media and experiencing life from what our world deems acceptable, the desires of the flesh would eventually lead me to His greatest ministry.

> Trust in the Lord with all your heart,
> and do not rely on your own insight.
> (Proverbs 3:5)

From the moment I walked away from blogging, I told God He was leading now, and I would listen. Well, I'm listening and trusting. Oh boy, am I trusting. This is my journey with social media, handling different trials that were thrown my way and how that battle I went through became my biggest blessing.

All the Whys!

M y goal and why I'm writing this book is to (1) help inform my daughters and your children on how to safely use social media because, let's face it, it's here to stay and will probably evolve even more over the next few years; (2) help people (of all ages) realize that God loves us, no matter our sins or how far you think you've fallen. The lies of our culture keep us trapped into thinking we can only trust ourselves or false idols. We become selfish and lose the ability to forgive and show compassion, leading to dehumanization toward others online and in person. It is a culture that is taking God and prayer out of our lives and making it easier to let evil in. The next few chapters will explain how I grew up, which I believe plays a huge role in my journey to become a fashion and beauty blogger and how redemption through Christ saved me and has enriched my life in ways I couldn't fathom.

Childhood

I grew up in a small town called Indian Land in South Carolina. In the eighties, there was only one stoplight and a gas station. We had to drive to neighboring towns for groceries and everyday essentials. We didn't have cell phones yet. Beepers and Gameboys were the hot electronics at the time and dial-up Internet was just beginning. My first year in college, 2001, I got a flip phone, and, oh, I thought I was hot stuff. There was no tracking my every step or seeing how fast I was driving my car. Thank goodness! It was simpler times. I loved how I grew up and wouldn't change a thing—well, except for when my brothers and my sister thought it would be funny to put a container of caterpillars under my bed, not realizing they could crawl out. Waking up from a dead sleep with them crawling on me, I'm sure I woke the neighborhood with my screams. Yeah, thanks, guys! I think I still have PTSD from that night. Caterpillars still freak me out, and I still can't get near one, although butterflies are acceptable.

I was and still am blessed with a loving family. Now that I'm an adult, looking back, I realize how lucky I am to have a mom and dad that loved me unconditionally, never trying to mold me into someone I wasn't, and never criticizing me for being myself. They loved and accepted both my siblings and me for who and what we were, flaws and all. As a parent now and looking back at how I was raised I'm in awe over how much love they showed us. I don't think, at the time, I knew how much my dad would play a significant role. Having such a positive male influence was something I took for granted when I was younger and didn't realize the impact it would have until I became a woman. I had so much love from my father that I didn't need another male to step into that role. I had the confidence to know what unconditional love looked like between my parents and with my siblings and me. Years later, when finding a partner to settle down with, I didn't look for someone to take care of me or fill a void. I was looking for someone who fit me and my personality, someone I could totally connect with on all levels, someone God made just for me. For that alone, I am eternally grateful. Even though we were all good kids, I am fully aware they probably prayed like crazy for my siblings and me during our high school years. My parents showed us what hard work looked like, how to love everyone, no matter their skin color, background, or views. They put God first in everything and made sure we went to church *every* Sunday. We thought, if it snowed, we wouldn't have to go. Nope, we were there. Probably how most teenagers feel, it was so annoying. I believed in God, learned my prayers when I needed to, and went through all the faith formation classes to get confirmed, so why was it so important to go every Sunday? I just wanted to sleep in one more day before Monday would rolled back around! It was even worse when I saw my friends doing fun things, but I had to go to church. As I write this now and look back on my teenage years, I'm so thankful they made me go because it provided me with good roots to fall back on when life gets hard. At the time though, it really sucked. Hind sight is twenty-twenty, I guess.

People who know me personally know I'm super competitive, hardheaded, and stubborn at times. Though some may look at that as a negative, there are a lot of positives that come along with it and also great for playing sports. I think being really competitive gives me the ability to look beyond pain or heartache and instead focus on victory. My competitiveness didn't develop over time. I was born with it. I remember, at a very young age, having a deep desire to win at anything I did. It didn't matter if it was playing in a T-ball game or competing in field day in elementary school. Wanting to win or learning how I could win and never stopping until I achieved it was probably why I was so involved in sports that continued on into my adulthood. I've retired at playing sports, but that drive is still there. Working as hard as I can and, more importantly, learning as much as I can to be the best in whatever endeavor I am pursuing is still a part of me to this day.

I started playing sports at a very young age, beginning with standard recreational teams, T-ball and basketball mostly. T-ball eventually turned into softball and basketball, fizzled out once I hit my peak height, and realized I was a little vertically challenged to still be playing. Although I can give you a run for your money at pig or horse, that's where my basketball skills stop.

Once I went to middle school and high school, I focused on volleyball and softball. I had fantastic coaches and teammates along the way. We were pretty bad ass back then. We earned that right by winning four South Carolina state championships in softball and one in volleyball. A lot of time, practice, sacrifice, blood, sweat, and tears went into getting to that level. Losing a game taught us more than winning. Yes, we were upset and probably had a very quiet bus ride home, but the next day we would show up to practice, ready to go over our mistakes, and learn from them. Losing a game only made us stronger and more determined to come back and win everything. It's not lost on me to realize how fortunate my coaches, teammates, and I were to stand in a circle and say the Lord's Prayer before every game. Even before our state championship game, we prayed and thanked God. To be a part of a team and experience four years of that happens only once in a lifetime. The drive to never quit was instilled into the entire team, and the support we had from all our coaches and parents is something I will always cherish.

Starting a Fashion and Beauty Blog

Throughout high school, a lot of what you hear are, What are you going to major in? Where are you going to school? What do you want to be? For some reason, we're supposed to have it all figured out by the ripe old age of eighteen years old. I thought I either wanted to be a nurse or dental hygienist. I eventually decided on dental hygiene for many reasons: (1) I knew I needed to stay from the neck up to prevent myself from gagging. I know my limitations, and thank God, He put people on this earth who don't mind changing bedpans or dealing with the oozes and smells that come from the neck down. (2) A typical work week is four days, with most holidays off. (3) The pay is fantastic coming right out of school. I wanted a career that could fully support myself financially but also be flexible if I decided to have kids one day. It seemed like a win in all areas, so I set off to become a dental hygienist after graduating high school.

With my dental hygiene license, I was fortunate to start working at a dental office that focused on the mouth-body connection and how it relates to our immune system. They provided me and my coworkers with a lot of extra education because they valued us as team members and knew the benefits of becoming the best in our field. The drive that I talked about earlier instantly kicked in, and I wanted to become the most knowledgeable hygienist, so I started learning all I could about the dental field. It's not that I want to outshine anyone; It's personal for me. I wanted to learn as much as I could so I could be the best, not only for myself but for my patients, my teammates, and the dentists. I was with this particular practice for almost four years until I had my first daughter and needed to work part-time. Life was changing, taking me down a different path, and it was time to move on. I truly value the time I spent there because it gave me the confidence to take the knowledge I learned and apply it to patients in other practices. It helped me to fully understand my field of work, how to explain different things to patients, and essentially how to grow a hygiene department.

The following years, I spent working part-time at a few different practices and eventually had my second child. I have a great marriage and family, great job, amazing friends. On paper, it seems like I would be extremely happy with the life I was living, so why would I want to change it? I was so blessed to be able to spend the majority of my time with my daughters. All was perfect. I knew God had blessed me and was truly happy. But around the time my youngest daughter was three, I started feeling like I wasn't where I needed to be. Something was missing from my life, and it didn't involve having another kid. It was a feeling that I was doing the wrong job, and my gut felt like

I was being called to do something else outside of dentistry. I'm sure, at some point in all our lives, we've had that feeling we're not where we're supposed to be. Most of us are taught at a very young age to think about what we enjoy doing, what areas our strengths are in, and lean toward that. I almost felt like I was in twelfth grade again, trying to figure out what to do with my life because my gut was telling me I was not in the right place. I thought and thought, talked to my husband, and consulted a few friends, and they all had the same response. I'm good at all things fashion and beauty. I started thinking I should start a fashion and beauty blog. I loved shopping, wearing new clothes, and styling others. In my head, I immediately thought, *Yes, that's it. That's what missing. I'm supposed to be doing what I love, and I have a love for fashion and beauty.* I thought, if I always get compliments on my outfits, hair, or makeup, why not get paid at the same time? I was fairly new to social media and saw these ladies making a nice living and having what looked like fantastic lives. Why not give it a chance? Not having experience in a certain field doesn't scare me because, surely, I could figure it out. I thought about it for a few more weeks, still consulting only myself and my husband. In the end, I decided to take a chance or take a leap of faith, because what could it hurt? In fact, I thought, becoming a blogger would be a good thing because I would be saving money in the long run by getting free clothes and getting paid for any products that I sold. I got excited for the endless possibilities of things that could happen along the way. In the forefront of my brain, I knew my hard work had never failed me at anything up to this point in life, so the thought of me not succeeding was nonexistent. It wasn't that I thought highly of myself, I just mentally always wanted to win. My competitiveness kept me focused on the outcome or end goal. So who or what could it hurt if I gave blogging a try, right?

Being very excited and a little nervous, I was ready to take on the next challenge in life, so I bought a domain, and Meganmariestyles was born. It was time to get to work!

How I Grew My Followers

After the excitement of having an official domain and web IP address is over, and reality kicks in, it all came crashing down that I had no idea what to do next. I remember writing down all the things I thought I needed to do to get up and running so I could post pictures and start making money. I spent hours researching how to create an actual web page, learned a lot about coding (which still confuses me) and how to navigate social media sights. I had no idea how to use or operate Instagram. I even had to look up how to upload a photo. I know that sounds crazy, but at that time, I was only on Facebook and had never used these other social media sites. So to say I was starting from scratch is a pretty accurate statement. I will save you the boring explanation regarding how to actually develop a website, but after a few weeks and lots of hours researching, my website was up and running. I completed the first big step. I learned enough about coding to put a decent website together. It definitely wasn't spectacular, and a professional could probably see that an amateur did it. But I was proud of it. It was easy to navigate and had all the links I needed to help maximize my income. I had a dear friend take some professional pictures that displayed how I would style different outfits so I could post links to where my followers could shop and buy everything I had on. Let me tell you, changing four or five times in the back of a car in the middle of a South Carolina summer is brutal. Hot is an understatement. More times than not, I didn't even notice until after the photos were taken for the day that I was drenched in sweat and in need of a shower.

Once I had the edited photos from my friend, I wrote my first blog article and hit post! I was ready for traffic to come to my page, collaborations to start, and possibly money to be flowing in. I laugh now, but, boy, was I wrong. It was crickets! Thankfully, I have very supportive friends who showed my post some love, but the outcome was definitely different than what I had envisioned. It stayed crickets until I started researching how IG's algorithm worked and figured out how to get people to engage with my post and gain followers. I switched to the business account on Instagram so I could see the analytics of each photo and video that I posted. It was eye-opening, to say the least. I learned that posting a photo doesn't mean your followers will see it. According to Instagram (and probably other social media outlets), if your post gets a lot of traction within the first fifteen minutes, they reward you by exposing your photos to more of your followers on their feed. It shows the newest content you've posted, whether it's a photo or video. To give you an example, at one point in my blogging career, I had over nine thousand followers. When I posted a photo or video, only two hundred people would be able to see it on their feed, unless the algorithm kicked in and distributed the photos to more followers. Without that algorithm, unless you actively searched for me, my posts probably wouldn't be seen. With trying to grow a business completely based online, that's pretty discouraging. If I'm being honest, it was definitely a blow to my ego. I knew it wasn't personally against me, but did it suck? Yes. But I was old enough to know it wasn't a reflection of my self-worth. I thought about my daughters or an impressionable young girl that feels like she's not getting enough likes on her photos and mentally doesn't know her self-worth yet. That can be pretty detrimental for someone at such a young age to experience. We'll dive more into that later, but that was my first red flag with social media. I made a mental note about what I saw and could see the problems with it, but I pushed it aside and kept diving deeper into the social media world. Again, I was growing my blog with the end goal being able to work and collaborate with different stores. I was going to keep pushing forward until I got to where I wanted to be. Nothing was going to stop me. I was focused.

When I was first starting out, I remember saying to my husband, "If only I could get to five hundred followers." I would see all these people with thousands and wanted to learn what I needed to do to get there. I eventually met a few ladies online who were doing the same thing, trying to increase engagement on their page. I was asked to join an IG group that communicated by DMs (direct message). I had no idea at first what it was and, after googling, found out it was a way to work around the algorithm to gain traction to your site and page. There usually would be ten to fifteen people in a group ranging in all ages, but we shared one goal: to increase our following, likes, and comments.

In return, it would increase exposure and potentially make more money. Here is how it worked: Whenever someone posted a photo, video, or blog post they would alert us in our DM group. We then would go like, comment, and sometimes save that photo to help that person get more exposure on IG. Again, it was all about how much traction your photo received in the first fifteen to twenty minutes. That would give it the best chance for it to be distributed for everyone to see. I can personally say, once I joined a few of these groups, my followers and exposure did start to increase. This process actually worked, and I found myself wanting to grow my followers faster. I became so focused on this one thing that I eventually started comparing my followers to other people's followers. I wanted to learn what they were doing to see if I could do the same thing. This only fueled my competitiveness with wanting to win at becoming an established social media influencer. I wanted to learn what else I could do to increase my exposure and get more followers. Again, this was a business I was creating. The more followers equaled more profit. I would always relate it to being in the dental field. When a dentist is first starting a practice and has no active patients, they have zero money coming in. The dentist needs bodies in the chair to work on, like I needed followers to my account. The more bodies in the chair, the more money they will make. The more followers I get, the more money I could make. Without me realizing, I got to a point where I became so focused on my followers and the analytics of each photo and video that it was all I thought about. There was no rest mentally. I started to obsess over it. Not knowing at the time what anxiety felt like, I was definitely experiencing something that was not normal. I never had doubts about my abilities, but my inner voice was starting to question if I was good enough. My inner voice was starting to become hyperaware of what others thought of me. My outer voice was still thriving though. I was starting to become good at compartmentalizing the stress that came along with constantly thinking how to grow my brand, get more likes and followers, and make money while juggling all other areas of my life. It was hard, and I handled it, but it probably wasn't the best thing for my well-being.

After being in the groups for an extended period of time, I was introduced to an app called Telegram. It was similar to the Instagram groups I was already a part of but on a much larger scale. You would upload your direct link to whatever you're posting and have hundreds of likes within minutes. Different groups had different rules, but the majority consisted of liking photos from the previous twelve hours. Once you caught up liking the other group member's previously posted photos, you could post your photo or video. I know that seems like a lot, but if spending ten or fifteen minutes liking other photos could result in you getting hundreds of likes and more exposure, then it was well worth it. I can say *a lot* of people do this, and I was part of the group of people who did. But I also saw people who had upward of 50–100K followers in these groups using it to enhance their exposure. You almost have to because you're a needle in a haystack since the number of social media influencers and bloggers have skyrocketed the past few years. It's like actors twenty years ago trying to make it in Hollywood. There were tons of people of all ages trying to increase their exposure and make it big acting in a film, but in reality, only a handful are successful. I think social media has grown into that. If you make it, at what cost did it take to get you there? What was I willing to do or what was I willing to sacrifice to be successful? In that stage of my life, quitting equaled failure. I don't quit just because something is hard; I dig deep and keep going. Eventually, I would have a win. So that's what I did; I kept going.

Being a part of the Instagram groups and using Telegram was helping but at a slower pace than I was expecting. I started seeing some of my friends I met through different Instagram groups post giveaways. Again, I had to do some research to figure out what's involved in launching a giveaway and needed to determine whether it was worth the expense. Some of the influencers already making it had enough followers that they usually funded the giveaways themselves, but we, little guys, just starting out needed some help. How it works: The giveaways ranged from high-end bags, trips to Disney World, or cash among other things, and the blogger running the giveaway would have a certain buy in amount with a certain amount of slots that other bloggers could register for. We would have to post at a certain time, like, and comment on everyone's post and repeat the process twenty-four hours later. At the end of the giveaway, someone would win a pretty nice prize. It was a win for everyone. I mean, who doesn't like free stuff? It was a way to get new followers fast, keep existing followers active on your site, and the host gained a profit for running the whole thing. More traction equaled more followers and new engagement to your page, which is very important if you want to work with the big brands. I decided to give it a try. It paid off because within the first twenty-four hours of posting about the giveaway, my account had jumped up almost 1K followers. *Wow,* I thought, *this is pretty amazing! This must be why everyone does giveaways on social media.* No matter how many followers you had, it was a great way to grow your brand. My thinking was that the forty dollars I spent to buy into and host the giveaway was a great way to market and promote myself. Looking back now, it seems silly. I was so focused and absorbed in getting people to follow me that I lost touch with reality. In that moment and during that time, all I saw was potential. All I thought about was myself. I kept going.

Around the time I hit 5K followers, brands started reaching out, and I was finally accepted to the *liketoknow. it* app. I didn't get accepted to the program the first time I applied a couple months earlier, but with the growth and engagement I was receiving on my account, I was finally accepted into the program. Like to Know It is an online platform where you post photos with links to where to buy the products and clothes you are wearing in your blog posts. If someone ends up buying something, either the product you posted or something else, you get a percentage of that sale. As long as the first click came from your account, you would get a portion of that transaction. A *click* means they were on your picture and clicked on the link to take them to the website where you bought the item. It really helped to increase my revenue while I was still growing. That was the fun part of blogging and what most people see; it looks easy and glamorous. People think it's easy to receive free merchandise or clothes from companies, but there is a lot of behind-the-scene work that people don't realize. People don't realize you may have to take thirty of the same photographs to pick just the right one that will make it to a post. People don't realize that it may have taken you days to weeks to market yourself to be able to work with a certain brand. Unless you are already bringing in enough money to hire an assistant, it's all up to you. I was consistently marketing and promoting myself. I wrote all my own blog posts for the website. My husband took my photos, and I edited them. It was a full-time job with the hours I was putting into this. It really was all I thought about. I would see the influencers I personally followed working with all these big brands, brands I thought I wanted to work with. It only made my drive stronger. I was determined to be in their shoes one day. I honestly didn't mind all the work I was putting into this endeavor because the growth in followers I saw every month kept me digging deeper to make it to my end goal. I was finally collaborating with lots of boutiques, Amazon companies, skincare lines, and jewelry lines. It was all starting to fall into place. All my hard work was starting to pay off. But again, at what cost?

My life became a routine each week. I would receive the clothes, think about how I was going to style them, and a good place to take photos. Generally, I would have a few outfit changes within one photoshoot to lessen the number of times my husband would have to spend his weekend taking pictures of me. If I could knock out three or four outfits in one shoot, that would provide enough content to cover a few weeks with professional-looking photos. Once I lined up my photographer, aka my husband, the only thing left was to promote and manage my engagement each day. I learned, if you always had an active video reel going, you would receive more traction to your page. They would expire within twenty-four hours, so I had to get creative and keep it going. It ended up being short reality clips of my life, from what I was doing in the morning, what vacation I was going on or what I was eating for dinner. I was comfortable filming and sharing my life with people, so it seemed natural. I was *always* on my phone working, but this was my daily life for two years. I was getting good, so I thought, with managing everything that was going on in my life.

While I was laser focused, working full-time, growing my social media accounts, I was still working as a dental hygienist, seeing patients two days a week. I also juggled taking care of the kids because my husband is the primary provider (financially) and worked in an office five days a week. To say I had a lot on my plate is an understatement. I was about a year and half into blogging when I figured out I was dealing with an extreme amount of anxiety. I became anxious the majority of the time. In previous months, I knew something different was going on internally, but at this point, I knew what it was; there was no question about it. It was a huge red flag for me because I've never experienced anything like this in my life. In some weird way, some of the anxiety developed from becoming an influencer, constantly feeling like I had to look perfect at all times of the day because you never know when you're going to take a picture or film a video or see someone that may know you. Mentally, if I didn't look perfect or seem perfect, I would be judged by others online or in person. My faith was strictly on myself and my reputation. I was trying to maintain focus and have control in all areas of my life, trying desperately to separate what my inner voices were telling me. They were all over the place. One minute I was thriving, I knew what my worth was, I was loved, I was beautiful and fearless. The next minute, I was questioning my self-worth. And if I'm good enough, I felt the people closest to me would look down on me if they saw me struggling with panic attacks. I was thinking I needed different filters to make my skin look better. It was like a tug-of-war going on inside my head, dealing with two inner voices that were competing against each other.

On top of feeling like I had to be or look perfect all the time and in the midst of trying to juggle each area and give the same amount of attention and focus to each of them, I started to worry about a number of things. I would worry I wasn't growing fast enough to work with the top brands. I would worry I wouldn't meet deadlines for companies sending me clothes. I would worry I wouldn't have my blog post ready by Friday. I would worry my husband and kids were possibly miserable driving around in the car with me so I could take photos and whether I was physically present enough for them. I was starting to question if I was the best hygienist for the dentist I currently worked with. I was worried and getting tired of holding my tongue because my patience was growing thin with an in-law who was consistently judging and criticizing me. All these things led me to have extreme anxiety. My inner voice at this point was definitely telling me I wasn't good enough. The tug-of-war was leaning more toward the darkness or negativity. Any light was slipping farther and farther away. For the first time ever in my life, I felt like I was failing. I felt like I was failing everyone because I was being stretched so thin, trying to remain and seem perfect and in control. Do I stay and fight trying to reach my goal of making it as a fashion and beauty influencer, or do I throw in the towel and walk away? I'm not a quitter, so I chose to stay and fight and try to deal with what I was experiencing. In the past, when going through challenging times, I knew that what was challenging me would eventually pass. I would just have to grin and bear it and wait until it passed, praying it would pass. No one around me (even my husband) had the slightest idea all this was going on internally. Like I said earlier, my outer voice was thriving and living her best life.

The perfect storm was brewing and about to come to a head; I just didn't know it at the time. I would soon be faced with two paths, and I would have to choose which one to take.

While managing my blog kept getting harder and harder, I was also met with unexpected challenges with my daughter in school that required more of my attention and time. My husband and I were starting to disconnect. I was still working two days a week, seeing patients, and the belittling from my in-law only increased. Deep down, I knew life shouldn't be this hard. I think I chose to ignore it all because I didn't want to fail at everything I had accomplished over the last two years. I didn't want to waste what I was in the midst of creating, and I didn't want my husband to think he wasted his time helping me to achieve it. But in the back of my mind, I was thinking it shouldn't be this hard.

Life continued on like normal—well, our new normal. I remember one morning while running on the treadmill, I broke down, crying and asking God for help. I was extremely happy with my life but very lonely on the inside. My anxiety at this point was full throttle, and I felt overwhelmed in most areas of my life. My inner voice had me thinking this is the way my life would be: lonely, angry, and feeling never good enough. My inner and outer voices were off course and not in sync. In my breakdown that particular morning, I remember asking God to help me make enough money so I can hire an assistant which, I thought, would solve all my problems. My thought process at the time was, if I had an assistant, I would have more time to focus on my kids and husband so we could reconnect. With an assistant I could focus on my patients at work and could be fully present in my own life. But it didn't happen. The exact opposite happened. I became even more overwhelmed with trying to be perfect while maintaining this imagine of what social media and working with different brands expected from you. I was angry at being disrespected and judged for years because I didn't fit into a box of what an in-law deemed acceptable. Not only was I being judged on a social media platform, but I was facing constant judgment and shame from someone who was supposed to love me, someone from my inner circle.

How do I forgive someone who sees nothing wrong with her behavior, and I'm supposed to monitor it for her? How will I ever trust her? My inner voice was telling me I'll never be accepted by this particular in-law, I'll never make it in blogging, I'll never be a good-enough mom or wife, and I'll never stop feeling anxious all the time.

Where are You, God? I felt very alone and left hanging to walk in this world alone. Yes, I was struggling but still trying my best to compartmentalize all the areas of my life, hoping things would get better one day. This was what I was supposed to be doing in life, right?

The Day My Life Changed

I grew up going to church, believing in God, but never knew Christ. It was like I was going through the motions because I knew I needed to. I thought being a Christian was going to church when it suited my family, dropping the kids off at Sunday school, and not passing judgment on others. I would only show up to church when it suited me and worked with my schedule. Looking back, it seems kind of silly. That's what I thought, but that's where I was. I had strayed so far away, thinking only of myself and what would benefit my family that I had lost sight of who was actually in charge. Maybe the problem was I didn't lose sight, I've never had the sight. I think I knew a religion not Christ. I knew God but controlled my own life. I was priority. I was alive but not truly living. I didn't realize it until I finally reached out to God in a different way one snowy night, in my car, while driving to a blogging function at Loft.

I had been prepping all day, getting myself ready, promoting, and marketing the event, looking at new items so I could have an idea of what pieces I was going to style together. The more the store sold, either in store or online, that evening, the better the chance of getting called back to host another event. I would do try-on sessions in store to post to my Like to Know it app, which added to the commission I would make. Try-on sessions are where I would style different outfits and film myself in a mirror, talking about how they fit, what size I was wearing for reference, and different ways to style the items. It was a great way to shop online because you could actually see the clothes on a person and get details on the fit of the clothes.

I spent all of thirty minutes with my girls that night before I kissed them, said goodbye, and headed on my way. While driving, I was feeling sad that I had left my family again, anxious to drive in the snow (I live in the south) but wanting the event to turn out well. I was also stressed because I knew all of Saturday would be spent taking new pictures of the clothes, editing them, and posting to my page. My family was not going to be happy. However, they would do it to support me because we're a team. I had stopped at a stoplight, zoned out, when suddenly I said out loud, "God if this is what you want for my life, I will do it. I will suck it up and keep marching forward. But if it's not, please show me. Send me a sign, and I will listen. I'm *listening*." That was the extent of my talk with God and continued on my way to Loft.

To be hosting, talking to different women, and helping them feel beautiful in their own skin, I would come alive. Every time I left an event like this, I was on a high. It's the only way I can explain it. I felt an immense feeling of happiness for the next few hours. It was a feeling of love because I felt and saw a glow come back into some of the faces of the women that I helped and talked with.

You could see their self-esteem return when they felt good in what they were wearing. All my hard work was finally paying off. I was happy and excited and couldn't wait to get home and tell my husband all about it.

I got home earlier than I expected since it was snowing, and everything shuts down quite early in the South when there is even a chance of snow. I immediately ran upstairs to say good night to my girls because I knew they were going to bed. Once I got in my oldest daughter's room, I sat on the bed and started asking her your typical mom questions: How did your night go? What did you, daddy, and your sister do? What did you eat for dessert (her favorite meal)? Without answering any of my questions, she looked me in my eyes and very calmly said, "Mommy, I wish you would stay home with us more. I wish you would get off the phone. I want you here with me." If you could stop time, I think it would feel like what I experienced in that moment. It was like I was frozen, and everything was happening all around me and then a rush of energy hit me. All of a sudden, I remembered my talk with God, that I was open and ready to listen, to show me some kind of a sign. All I could do in that moment was hug and hold her while fighting back tears that would soon be overflowing. I didn't want to let go because, in that moment, I knew God was working through my daughter. Maybe He had to use her because it would be the only way I would listen. That night, everything changed. I still can't explain the feeling, but every fiber in my being knew it was Him and knew my life would be different going forward. I knew I wasn't in control anymore. There was an immense amount of peace that I felt, realizing things were going to be different, that I was going to be different. The only thing I could get out of my mouth without completely losing it was I loved her very much, and I was going to make a change. I kissed her good night and headed back into my room, where my husband was waiting.

I walked back into my room with tears flowing. My husband was probably thinking I was finally losing it because I was just excited about the night. I sat on the bed and said I have to quit blogging. Quitting in the middle of something was a new experience for me. Talk about feeling like a failure. I had a flood of emotions going through me—sadness mainly because I didn't realize the extent of my family's loneliness while I was blogging. Letting go of all my hard work I had invested over the past two years was a hard pill to swallow. However, I also felt a calmness come over me, as if God was spiritually comforting me, trying to tell me it was going to be okay. As I was crying, trying to get out the words to fill my husband in on what I just experienced, I saw a little smile on his face, a smile that told me he didn't think I was a failure, and in that moment, that's all I needed to be okay with my decision. I think, deep down he was as happy as my daughter to hear the news. Almost like this whirlwind of a storm we were in would soon be settling down, and we would get our life back. The rest of the night we talked—well, I talked (poor guy) most of the night because reality was hitting. I was nervous, scared, relieved, and anxious all at the same time. I knew people would have no clue or understand why I was walking away. I didn't fully understand myself what was going on at the time other than I told God I was listening, and He was leading. The next morning, after getting the girls to school, I came home and filmed my last video. It took several times trying to make it through without having the ugly cry, but eventually I got through it. Once I hit that post button, there was no turning back. I stared at the button for what felt like minutes, having flashbacks of all the fun I had along the way, remembering only the good times, and the amazing people I met. I just stared at it, contemplating whether I should follow what I want or follow God's plans. This was it. This was the end of my storm, and I had to make a choice on which path I would choose. Do I have faith to follow something I can't see or understand, or should I keep trusting in only myself and following what has grown to be a normal way of life? I thought of what transpired the previous night and immediately hit post. I didn't know what was coming next. That was the last post from Meganmariestyles. I had made my choice.

Life after Meganmariestyles

To be honest, I wasn't sure what God wanted me to do next. I just continued working part-time as a hygienist and tried to help my daughters learn how to navigate through school. I spent my days enjoying my family now that I had a lot of extra free time. Not knowing what God wanted me to do, I just kept trusting that eventually, when it's the right time, He would let me know. This was new for me, almost a different life. I was accustomed to being focused on an outcome I wanted, and to let that go felt weird and scary. It's hard to put into words, but something deep within me knew it was going to be okay. I felt almost relieved that I didn't have to do it by myself anymore. The weight I was carrying, some of the anxiety I was feeling, was slowly going away. It felt like someone was removing that part of me that was created over the last few years. It could be a coincidence, but that alone made me excited to see what my life could be like with God leading.

The beginnings of His plan came unexpectantly and was something definitely not on my radar. It started when my oldest was going through First Communion at church. We were at rehearsal, and something came over me that made me want to volunteer at church. I initially wanted to start small by handing out flyers after church or helping out with festivals. I laugh now because someone else had other plans for me. When I asked the faith formation leader that day if anyone needed help, her response was immediate. "We need Sunday school teachers," she said. *Wow*, I thought in my head, definitely not what I was envisioning. I quickly responded with, "Are you sure I could teach? I'm a dental hygienist and have no teaching background other than with my kids." In my head, I was also telling myself, "What the heck are you doing? You believe in God, but that's the extent of your godliness. Do they even know you can count on one hand how many times you went to church this year? Oh boy, what am I getting myself into?" This conversation with the faith formation leader and the thoughts going through my head lasted all of twenty seconds. I politely said I would think about it and get back to her, hoping my facial expressions didn't give away to what I was battling inside.

A few weeks later, I was still unsure of my answer. I had preconceived limitations and was very nervous and uncomfortable with saying yes. I consulted or told my husband, mom, and dad about possibly becoming a Sunday school teacher. I think they all had the same reaction as myself, "Are you sure?" I was extremely nervous to be out of my element, but I remembered what I told God in the car on the way to Loft that night. I told Him I was listening and would follow Him, but He would need to guide me. Once that thought ran through my mind, I immediately emailed the faith formation leader and told her *yes*! On that day, I became a first-grade catechist, also known as a Sunday school teacher. After taking a few courses and getting approved from the diocese to teach children, it was time to figure out what the heck a first-grade catechist should teach. I even asked God if He knew what He was getting Himself into with me. I'm kind of loud and pretty opinionated, but He had a plan. It was my job to listen and trust that He knew what He was doing. Looking back, it seems so crazy to think I was nervous I couldn't do it. Once I got out of my own way and realized how easy it was to make a lesson plan, I began to enjoy it.

Going into my first year, I didn't know what to expect; I just knew I wanted the class to have fun while learning about God's love and Jesus. In complete honesty, I was relearning about it as well. It had been so long since I picked up a Bible, and to be able to make lesson plans every week really helped me introduce God back into my life, something I previously didn't understand was missing. I believed in God and grew up in the faith, but I wasn't truly living it. The more the weeks went on and the more I taught, the more I had a feeling of gratitude—gratitude because I could see small areas in my life starting to change for the better. I found myself wanting to volunteer more inside and outside of the church. I had an overwhelming feeling to help people. I was becoming less selfish with my time. Once I removed myself from being the main priority, I started seeing that a lot of people needed help, not just physical but emotional help. I found that just sitting and talking with people and showing love can go a long way. I started tithing for the first time ever in my life and still do every time I get paid. I could feel God changing things within myself, like a light was starting to overcome a darkness I didn't realize was present. The more I saw positive change within certain areas of my life, the more I wanted to keep going, having not a clue where I was going or where I was being lead. That inner voice that once was telling me I would always be anxious, I would never be a good enough mom or wife was slowly being replaced with love, that I'm loved. My inner voice was starting to appreciate life and what's been given to me. How thankful I am to be living this life that God gave me. How thankful I am to be able to help people. My inner voice was slowly starting to match the outer voice.

As the months went by, I was developing a new normal in my life. My daughters were thriving and overcoming the challenges they were experiencing. I was continuing to teach faith formation and was still working part-time as a hygienist. Life was good until I started to get that feeling again that I wasn't where I needed to be. After everything I was experiencing, I was still clueless as to where that was supposed to be. I felt confused and annoyed that God would bring me all this way and just leave me hanging. There had to be a reason. I thought back over the last few months and started to remember what He has already brought me out of and decided to stay focused and trust His plan. The feeling I was struggling with was the same feeling I got all those years prior before I started my blog. This time, instead of consulting myself to figure it out, I consulted God. I simply prayed and asked, "What do You want me to do? What do You want for my life?" I just had to be patient. I kept following and pursuing Him and waiting until the timing was right. Patience is something I'm learning to have and, to this day, still struggle with, but I've learned God's time is definitely at a different pace than mine.

I find listening to God's voice is hard sometimes, and you don't get an answer right away. It may be just me, but on most occasions, I would have to determine if it's God speaking, me speaking, or the devil speaking. I have made mistakes along the way trying to decipher which I should listen to. It's like in the old movies where you had a devil on one shoulder, an angel on the other, and you're in the middle. It can be very challenging, especially in the culture we live in today. I remember reading that if something is from God, it will come to you. I'm not saying to just sit back and wait to be served your blessings; what I'm saying is you won't find yourself fighting so hard for something that is having a negative effect on your life. If it's from God, there will be an inner calmness, not raging anxiety. There will be hard work and setbacks at times, but it will work out according to His plan, and you will not fail.

> Fear not, for I am with you, be not dismayed, for I am your God; I will strengthen you, I will help you, I will uphold you with my victorious right hand. (Isaiah 41:10)

Knowing there was a bigger plan at play and not understanding what it was made it hard for me to determine what I should do or the next steps I needed to take.

I found myself questioning everything again. Then something inside me clicked. The moment I started to question things is the moment I began taking back control. Control is a hard one for me. I find myself to this day letting go of control. But when I get scared or nervous, I find myself trying to take it back. Gosh, it's so hard. It's so easy to get distracted by multiple things and drift...again and again. This particular time, I caught it and quickly said to myself, "Not today. You're not pulling me away from all the great things God has done and is continuing to do in my life." I lost focus without even realizing it. Being aware of when you do and getting back on track is the solution. Allowing myself grace was a game changer in the pursuit to something I still had no understanding of. The only thing I had and understood at this time in my life was an inner calmness and a feeling that everything was going to work out. It's an inner calmness unlike anything I have ever felt before. I can't fully put into words, but it's something I never want to stop having. That's one of the main ways I can tell when I start drifting away, that calmness subsides, and anxiousness starts to slowly creep in again. When I feel that, it's an indicator I need to reevaluate and see if I'm living for God or myself. In most cases, it's for myself because it's second nature for me.

I was learning and growing so much while waiting on what I should do next. I didn't know if I was waiting on a feeling or someone to cross my path. I had no clue. I was just waiting, having a feeling I would know when it's time to move and take my next step.

I think it happened months later, after asking Him what He wanted me to do. When I knew, I knew. I knew on that day and in that moment, deep down in my gut. There was no questioning the situation. I knew what my next step needed to be. Now that was God speaking. The overwhelming calmness I felt allowed me to understand that it would be okay when I had to tell my husband I was stepping back from my permanent hygiene position, and he would financially be taking over paying all the bills. The calmness of not having a plan but knowing something better was coming. The calmness that everything was going to be okay. I wasn't sure how, but my gut knew to trust, and He would succeed any dreams I had dreamed of. So I did. It was time to move. Through tears, I gave my boss a four-month notice. I laughed, but I wanted to give him plenty of time to find someone. He was so good to me, and I felt bad for leaving, but it was my time to move on. By December 2020, I was saying my goodbyes to an awesome team and patients I had met along the way and started my new journey. I've had a job since I was fifteen years old, and this was the first time in my life I was leaving a job, not having something else lined up. I can envision what Abraham must have thought when he was told to leave his homeland in Haran and travel to a land in which God did not tell him yet. He was leaving the only life he had ever known, a life he was probably comfortable in but trusted God to show him the way. He eventually went to the land of Canann but in verse 1–2 from Genesis 12: 1–9 he was only told to leave, not knowing where to go. I find myself relating to that scripture. Yes, I know I'm not Abraham. I was comfortable. I had a great schedule working two days a week. Why would I want to leave? I still don't know, but something was telling me it's time. It's my job to have faith and trust knowing he has a purpose and plan. I'm in His hands, and He won't fail me. God used my daughter months earlier to get my attention. When I promised Him I would listen, I meant it. When I give my word to something, I will follow through.

As I was on my journey, knowing somehow it was going to be okay, my husband started having concerns about finances. This was new territory for us. I've always paid for my car, groceries for our family, and other odds or ends, things that our family needed. That money was now gone. He had every right to be nervous because I would imagine he felt a lot of pressure—pressure to know he would now be solely responsible for paying for everything. I just remember telling him, "It's going to be okay. It's going to work out. I just can't tell you how." I could tell that was not reassuring to him and probably made him more nervous because he likes having a plan too. He decided to trust me as I was trusting God. Three months into leaving my job, I got an email from my periodontist, Dr. Brenda Lopez, asking if I knew someone who could help fill in. Not knowing I had walked away from my permanent position months earlier, I emailed back and said I could help. The hours and schedule were perfect because I could choose what would fit my family's schedule. What I thought years earlier about how my work schedule couldn't get any better, well it just got better. How lucky am I that I get to work with an exceptional periodontist and the nicest people while being a mom and putting my family first. It was not luck; that was God. It was Him providing for my family along the way while on this journey. I guess you can say I was in the desert, traveling to my promised land after He had rescued me from my own Egypt, a slavery of a different kind. I'm currently two years into filling in for that office and counting my blessings every day. I still don't know where He is taking me or what His plans are for me. Besides my husband, no one knew what I was experiencing. I wasn't fully sure myself on what it was but wanted to keep it between me and God. I didn't want opinions of others to get in the way of His word. I didn't want anyone trying to convince me to turn away from God and have doubt in myself. He had work to do within me, and I needed to stay focused, quiet, and listen.

Being fully present with your kids is crucial.

Train up a child the way he should go. (Proverbs 22:6)

For the first time ever in my children's life, I was fully present. I wasn't distracted or on my phone. I took electronics away, except for certain allotted times. We started spending quality time together, and I could be very involved in their school academics. Their emotional well-being had changed in just a few short months. I could see not only God changing me but also my family. True happiness was returning. We were no longer in different parts of the house doing our own thing. We were more united as a family. Church became a priority, no more excuses as to why we couldn't make it. As long as we were in town, we would be there. One particular Sunday, in the bulletin, staring me right in the face, was a huge advertisement regarding an upcoming women's Bible study. The thought crossed briefly that maybe I should check it out. The thought was brief because I never thought about it again. A few weeks later, I was reading the bulletin while waiting on church to start, and there it was again, registration for the women's Bible study. This time, it was a take-home flyer with the schedule on it. I took it out of the bulletin and just stared at it, thinking to myself, *Should I sign up?* This time, the thought lasted more than a few seconds. I laughed and said to myself, "All right, God, You have my attention. You know I'm hardheaded, and it may take a few times to get to me, but I hear You. I'm listening now." The following Monday, being scared and completely out of my element, I emailed the leaders and bought the book for the class. I had signed up for my very first Bible study. I, someone who had drifted so far away from the church, was now about to attend a Bible study. Who would have thought?

Walking into the first class was intimidating. I had no clue what I was doing and was embarrassed by the fact I didn't know the Bible. I've previously tried to read it but never really understood it. Following a lesson plan and teaching first graders in faith formation seemed like a walk in the park compared to what I thought I was about to experience. As the class was getting started, we all introduced ourselves and stated why we were there. Oh boy, here we went! I was up next, and what the heck was I going to say? I started sweating just thinking about the judgment that might come from these ladies. They were twenty to thirty years my senior, and I thought I might be judged for not knowing the Bible as well as they did. When it was my turn, I went with honesty. While trying to speak with calmness, I stated my name and told everyone I wasn't sure why I was there. I felt God calling me to this class, so here I was. He had a purpose, and I was here to figure out what that was for me. I stopped and waited to see if I should go crawl into a hole. The response was the exact opposite of what I thought. The overwhelming love and acceptance these ladies showed me was incredible. No matter our age, I found we were all on different journeys to grow closer to God or to find our purpose through God. If I learned anything from that day, it was to not judge a book by its cover. I had a preconceived notion of what I thought Bible study was, and I was wrong, extremely wrong. There was so much love and acceptance among the group. It felt safe; I felt safe. It gave me the reassurance that it was okay if I didn't know all the Bible stories. It was okay that I was at the beginning of my journey. It was okay to feel whatever I was feeling. We were there to grow and walk on our own path while supporting each other along the way. I'm so glad God got me out of my own way to experience it.

Bible study met once a week for twenty-two weeks. During those weeks, we studied the Gospel of John. Week after week, chapter after chapter, I was slowly seeing things differently. For the first time in my life, I was starting to understand the Bible. I noticed a lot of what happened within the gospel is still happening today. It goes all the way back to the Old Testament with Moses freeing the slaves. God had an easier time getting the Israelites out of Egypt and freeing them from slavery than taking Egypt out of the Israelites. They wandered around for forty years, lost in the desert, with only a few making it to the promised land. They got stuck thinking about how things used to be in Egypt. They got scared and started to rebel after hearing stories about what was happening in Canaan. They had drifted and lost faith on who was leading them, the same God who freed them from slavery. They got stuck remembering what used to be instead of what could be or what is to be. Think about that and see if you can relate it to your life. I know I sure can. Do we get stuck living in the past, thinking of only what was or what used to be? Do we get stuck thinking life will never change and will always be overwhelmed with anxiety, depression? Do we get stuck thinking we aren't good enough, which can hold us back from living our best life? Are we scared to let go of our control and have faith? I started to learn that if you don't have God at the forefront, you will stay paralyzed in your current predicament, keeping you wandering in your own desert—meaning, if you're not walking with Christ, you could stay stuck in what used to be and may miss what's to come and the wonderful life God has promised all of us.

I kept having ah-ha moments. I could directly relate to some of the situations in the Bible. Some of the stories within the Gospel of John, I could see myself in. It was all starting to make sense in a way it hadn't before. My perspective on what I had gone through with my journey in the blogging world and my relationship with an in-law of mine had drastically changed. I was learning that through God comes love, through God comes forgiveness, and through God comes redemption. Our repentance and redemption are directly through Jesus Christ. Learning about evil and how important it was for Jesus to save us made me look at myself differently. I started to realize the Bible is not just something you read for fun; it's a manual on how to fight against evil and how to love through it. I've sinned so many times that I've lost count, but I know His love for me goes way deeper than my sins. He loves us so much that He sent His only Son to be a sacrificial lamb so He could have a direct relationship with us. Jesus Christ made that happen. I started to forgive myself for my own sins and the guilt I had for not putting God first. I started to forgive my in-laws. I didn't feel as much resentment or anger anymore. I started to feel sadness because this is what a relationship looks like if God's not leading it. You stay stuck in hurt, anger, and resentment with no way out. Evil had been winning the battle in my life, keeping me trapped. But God had different plans, the first of them being getting me into Bible study.

I'm finding the Bible is a book about how real people dealt with evil and how God showed them His love. The same evil is still happening today, just in a more modern way. I never realized it until I started to read and understand the Bible. I had a lot of life questions at that point and found most of the answers through the Bible. Every time I completed a Bible study lesson, a new light bulb would go off, and I started gaining a new perspective. I was beginning to understand that my ego and selfishness were part of the problem. My ego wouldn't let me quit blogging because I didn't want to be a failure. My ego wouldn't let me admit I was drowning with carrying the weight of the world on my shoulders. My ego wouldn't let me ask for help because I didn't want to look weak. My selfishness had my family spending most weekends taking photos of me for my blog. My selfishness kept me constantly glued to my phone because I was more concerned with getting extra likes or comments on a photo. My selfishness was putting my faith within myself and not in God. In my selfishness, I thought, just because I was baptized and was a Christian, I was good. This was a result of solely relying on myself and consulting only myself my entire life. If I kept doing life my way, I would either need to be medicated to help control the anxiety, or I would eventually be self-medicating with alcohol or anything else that would numb the reality of life. Deep down, before stepping back from blogging, I knew life didn't have to be this hard but didn't know how to get myself out. I felt trapped. I thought I needed to "clean" myself up before allowing God in or having God accept me. It's the exact opposite; He wanted me exactly how I was: broken and scarred.

I remember thinking when I started the journey of solely listening to God that I was afraid of what others might think or the backlash that could happen. We are living in a world where God is somehow offensive to some people. I'm blessed with a husband who loves me unconditionally and is always there, rooting for me to become my best self. His never-ending support essentially helped me stay focused while I was just beginning my journey. Before the women's Bible study, I was afraid of what my friends might think. I was afraid I would lose lifelong friends because I was becoming a different person. They had known me most of my life, one way, where I was Christian but had no relationship with God, and to change would possibly make me look crazy or weird. I was caring so much more about what they thought rather than what God thought. I liked my life and didn't want to lose any friends over me taking a different path. I thought I would miss parts of my old life and the social scene. But I was willing to take that leap because, in my gut, I didn't want that calmness I felt to go away, and I knew something so much bigger was waiting. I still get nervous and unsure at times, but I am reminded about the promise I made God that night in my car, the promise I would listen and His promise He would show me the way.

What do you think? If a man has a hundred sheep, and one of them has gone astray, does he not leave the ninety-nine on the hills and go in search of the one that went astray? And if he finds it, truly, I say to you, he rejoices over it more than the ninety-nine that never went astray. (Matthew 18:12–13)

But I say, walk by the Spirit, and do not gratify the desires of the flesh. For the desires of the flesh are against the Spirit, and the desires of the Spirit are against the flesh; for these are opposed to each other, to prevent you from doing what you would. (Galatians 5:16–17)

And you he made alive, when you were dead through the trespasses and sins in which you once walked, following the course of this world, following the prince of power of the air, the spirit that is now at work in the sons of disobedience. Among these we all once lived in the passions of our flesh, following the desires of our body and mind and so we were by nature children of wrath, like the rest of mankind. But God, who is rich in mercy, out of the great love with which he loved us, even when we were dead through our trespasses, made us alive together with Christ (by grace you have been saved). (Ephesians 2:1–5)

These verses hold true in every aspect of my life. I had gone astray. I got caught up in our culture and wanting things the flesh desires: money, materialistic things, and a higher status on social media, thinking I could have both and selfishly asking for more clothes, more followers or likes, and making more money. I was living for this world while praying for God to fix all my problems. A light bulb went off in my head. You can't have it both ways. To truly walk in the Spirit, your desires can not be what our flesh wants them to be. No wonder I felt like God didn't hear me all those months ago, the time I felt alone, left hanging to walk through life by myself. It wasn't that He wasn't with me or didn't hear me. I was just too consumed with living for what this world offers and praying those things would change. What I thought I needed to bring happiness and peace back into my life was complete opposite of what God knew had to be done. God didn't t care what top brands I wanted to work with. God doesn't care about my status on social media. He needed to cancel out all the noise around me so I could focus because I was the lost sheep that needed to be rescued. I understood now why He wanted me to join that class. My purpose of joining that class was to learn to hear God's voice on a deeper level and to understand His purpose for my life while on this earth. It all started with asking Him for help and learning to listen during prayer. I needed not to just talk about it; I needed to be about it. Take action, and start living life selflessly. Little by little, day by day, month by month, all the fears I had of what others would think slowly went away, and I started to care only of what God thought. I started to recognize what evil sounded and looked like. Most importantly, I was learning how to rebuke it. The devil can use people to influence you or could use what you're watching and listening to. The devil doesn't change but *you* will. Completely unaware and sometimes being rewarded, keeping you bound and blinded. When you start to have a relationship with God, evil comes knocking, and half the time you won't even know it. The one thing evil can't overcome is God. He holds all the power and can't be defeated. I was starting and ending my day in prayer, thanking Him for how far He's brought me and areas I still needed help with. I was learning that having a relationship with Him was drastically different than just believing in God and going to church when it suited myself or my family. As I continued my path following my faith, I also found my husband and kids were starting down their own spiritual path. Even though we're a family unit, we're all on different journeys while walking on our path. It was a start of something and something that's still growing. It's a special thing we're experiencing together. It didn't happen overnight, but the more I trust Him, the more He provides. To hear people say they walk on faith not sight—I fully understand that now.

All areas of my life were drastically improving. One of which my husband noticed first was my shopping habits. I found myself not having the desire to shop unless it was necessary. That's huge for me! I had spent the majority of my life shopping the newest trends, buying some skin care product to make me look younger than thirty-nine or a new pair of boots that were a shade lighter or darker than what I already had. You name it; I probably was buying it. I don't know if I had an addiction to shopping or I just enjoyed being in new clothes. Ultimately, I think that's why I wanted to start a fashion and beauty blog. I was good at styling and enjoyed shopping. Therefore, blogging was a way to make money and get free clothes. We all know how that ended, but ending the blog didn't stop my shopping habits. We were halfway through the Bible study class when I noticed it. I remember the day very vividly when I first noticed I had no desire to shop. The Nordstrom sale was approaching, and I had an email reminding me that card members had early access to the sale. Years passed, I would have already had a wish list going, but this time it was empty. As I sat there, staring at my Nordstrom email, it hit me. It had been months since I went shopping. Other than the necessities that my family needed, I had bought nothing for myself. It felt good because I felt fulfilled—fulfilled in a way I had never known before. I sat there quietly with tears falling, thanking God for all He was doing in my life. For some, this may sound silly because it's just shopping, but for me it was bigger than that. I was becoming aware that I shopped to be happy. It wasn't that my life was unhappy, but shopping made everything better. If I was happy, I shopped. If I was stressed, I shopped. If I was sad, I shopped. If I was angry, I shopped. I was filling a void I didn't even realize I had.

This upcoming verse is a long one, but I see myself in that Samarian woman, not the married five times part but the thirsty part. The Samarian woman was thirsty and not just for water. She was always trying to fill a void and was filling it with different men. I was filling mine with shopping. I didn't even realize it until God started transforming my life. I would encourage you to read the entire John, chapter 4, but below is a segment from it.

> There came a woman of Samaria to draw water. Jesus said to her, "Give me a drink." For his disciples had gone away into the city to buy food. The Samaritan women said to him, "How is it that you, a Jew, ask a drink of me, woman of

Samaritans." Jesus answered her, "If you knew the gift of God, and who it is that is saying to you, 'Give me a drink,' you would have asked him, and he would have given you living water." The woman said to him, "Sir, you have nothing to draw with, and the well is deep; where do you get that living water? Are you greater than our father Jacob, who gave us the well and drank from it himself, and his sons, and his cattle?" Jesus said to her, "Everyone who drinks of this water will thirst again, but whoever drinks of the water that I shall give him will never thirst; the water that I shall give him will become in him a spring of water welling up to eternal life." (John 4:7–14)

The only thing I had done differently in my life the last year and a half was accept God and Jesus Christ into my life. I asked for help, repented for my sins, and was committed to listening, learning, and trusting in Him. Other than that, everything else remained the same. When I realized I had no desire to shop and was fulfilled more in my life than I had ever been, it made me fully understand what Jesus meant when He told that Samaritan woman that if she knew God's gift and asked for water, He would have given her living water, and she would not thirst again. She would have eternal life. I asked God to step in and help me on my way to Loft that night. I asked God to lead the way, and I would listen. My void, which was shopping, was no longer there. I was living, truly living. All I had to do was ask and seek Him, putting action toward whatever He is calling me to do. What would normally have been me spending my time shopping the latest fashions turned into volunteering more time at the senior center and other places that needed help. The more I walked with Christ, the less selfish I became. I've experienced what the Holy Spirit can do in a person's life. The moment I asked God for help is when my life started to change. It was clear; I wasn't in control, something I couldn't see or fully wrap my brain around. I found myself being intrigued on the how and why. How does the Holy Spirit work? How can it completely change my life and my inner voice, and why did it choose me? I like knowledge. I like to be able to research and explain something. I like living in truth and not going off what someone is telling me. I wanted to find answers to all the questions I had. Where do I begin? I started with the living Word of God, The Bible.

The Holy Spirit is part of the Holy Trinity. The Holy Trinity consists of God, Jesus, and the Holy Spirit. There's a great mystery behind it. It goes beyond our own understanding, and we can't interpret it ourselves. The more I began to study and research the Holy Spirit, the more I felt myself growing closer to understanding and ultimately beginning to know God. The Holy Trinity (God, Jesus, and the Holy Spirit) are one because they are fully God. The Spirit is sent to us to help us love. The Spirit is sent to show His love for us so we can truly be happy deep within our hearts and soul. The Spirit was sent to us to be able to have a relationship with Him (God) and to help show us our purpose on earth. What some people may say is intuition could actually be the Holy Spirit working and guiding you.

> But the counselor, the Holy Spirit, whom the Father will send in my name, he will teach you all things, and bring to your remembrance all that I have said to you. (John 14:26)

How did we come to receive the Holy Spirit?

> Then Jesus was led by the Spirit into the wilderness to be tempted by the devil. (Matthew 4:1)

> The Spirit immediately drove him out into the wilderness. (Mark 1:12)

I would imagine, in the time Jesus walked this earth, the disciples would have thought He was following his intuition, His gut or inner voice to go into the wilderness to be tempted by the devil. I would also imagine Jesus was probably unsure why He was going up there for forty days. He had the Spirit living inside of Him and guiding Him to do so. In *John 14:16–17*, it says,

> And I will pray the Father, and he will give you another counselor, to be with you forever, even the Spirit of truth, whom the

world cannot receive, because it neither
sees him nor knows him; you know him,
for he dwells with you and will be in you.

Jesus knew He had the spirit of God with Him. He trusted blindly and went solely off of faith. God knew His plan, and Jesus knew His purpose. What was so incredible about Jesus's purpose and how much He sacrificed for us is we now get to experience that direct relationship with God, and that comes through the Holy Spirit. Because of Jesus, we get to have the Holy Spirit dwelling inside of us. Because of Jesus, we get to experience spiritual gifts that were placed in all of us.

Now there are varieties of gifts, but
the same Spirit; and there are varieties of
service, but the same Lord, and there are
a varieties of working but is the same God
who inspires them in everyone. To each
is given the manifestation of the Spirit
for the common good. (1 Corinthians
12:4–7)

We all have different spiritual gifts living within us but can only access them if we are walking in the spirit of God and not living according to the flesh and false idols. Can you imagine our world if we all lived according to our spirit, the one from God? What an incredible place that would be!

As I'm doing my research on the Holy Spirit, I came across the parable Jesus told the crowd by the sea. And He told them many things in parables, saying,

> A sower went out to sow. And as he sowed, some seeds fell along the path, and the birds came and devoured them. Other seeds fell on rocky ground, where they had not much soil, and immediately they sprang up, since they had no depth of the soil, but when the sun rose they were scorched; and since they had no root they withered away. Other seeds fell upon thorns and the thorns grew up and choked them. Other seeds fell on good soil and brought forth grain, some a hundredfold, some sixty, some thirty. He who has ears, let him hear. (Matthew 13: 3–9)

Let's break that down by the four different sowers of seeds because essentially, we are the different seeds.

Verse 3: "Some seeds fell along the path, and the birds devoured them". Some of us hear the Word of God but never took the time to understand it before the evil one (the devil) comes and snatches what God placed on our hearts. Meaning we never had a chance to make it onto the path before evil stepped in and devoured us keeping us from ever hearing God's Word.

Verse 5: "Other seeds fell on rocky ground, where they had not much soil, and immediately they sprang up, since they had no depth of soil, but when the sun rose they were scorched and since they had no root they withered away." Those are people who made it to the path and receive God's Word with excitement, but as soon as life gets hard or trials come up pertaining to God and His Word, they quickly fall back. Rejecting and dismissing anything associated with God.

Verse 7: "Other seeds fell upon thorns, and the thorns grew up and choked them." These people also made it to the path, they hear God's Word but are too caught up living for this world; the riches, the false idols. They never reach their full potential or purpose because they're letting society control them. These people bear no fruit because His Word is being smothered by the cares for this world.

Verse 8: "Other seeds fell on good soil and brought forth grain, some a hundredfold, some sixty, some thirty. He who has ears, let him hear." These people hear God's Word and fully understand it. They understand the power of God and want other people to hear and receive the power too. They aren't ashamed and stand in His truth.

Which seed do you fall into?

I personally was the seed that fell upon the thorns. I would be lying to myself if I didn't realize at a young age, I like nice things, new cars, new clothes, the glitz and the glamour. I was drawn to those things. I was once a little seed that fell upon the thorns and was there for most of my life, blogging on social media took it to a new extreme. The thorns quickly began to spread and choke any hope of spreading God's Word and living in His truth.

In 1 John 2:15–17, it says, "Do not love the world or the things in the world. If anyone loves the world, love for the Father is not in him. For all that is in the world, the lust of the flesh and the lust of the eyes and the pride of life, is not of the Father but is of the world. And the world passes away, and the lust of it; but he who does the will of God abides forever."

When we live for the spirit of this world, could that be why we experience anxiety, depression, and confusion as to who or what we are, trying to live up to the standards of what this world deems acceptable, pretty, smart, or what's right verses wrong? We're left wondering around, lost, searching for something to help us identify who we are and doing whatever we see fit. When we live of this world's spirit, we forget we are all children of God. We drift and forget who made us and who knew us before we were born. We get lost. Look at the world around you. Every day I hear of someone talking about the rise in mental health concerns and the increased rate in depression and suicide, especially among kids. Our country was founded on God. And over the last century, God somehow has been removed from almost everything. I think it warrants a discussion as to why we have a lot of adults and kids struggling mentally or dealing with some sort of mental health problem. Could it be we're living in this world's spirit? Could it mean who we're watching we are all becoming? Could it mean we're too focused on ourselves and our own desires? Could it mean we've lost the teachings of God's word that the Holy Spirit isn't being invited into our hearts and minds? Could it be that we all are Christians but have drifted so far away, living for what this world desires (money, power, and pride)? Could it be, in our drift, we've forgotten to teach our children what it truly means to live and walk with Christ? I don't know, but I do know the Bible is full of stories about people who experienced and dealt with the same things we're seeing in this modern-day world, stories about selfishness, anger, power, and pride but also stories about faith, hope, and trust. I do know that we will stay stuck in whatever we're going through if each person continues living their life for what they think is right and just. Our world will stay in this spiritual battle if we don't renew our mind and start living for God.

> Do not be conformed to this world but be transformed by the renewal of your mind, that you may prove what is the will of God, what is good and acceptable and perfect. (Romans 12:2)

God is the only one who can do that, no one else— no influencer, no professor, no journalist, no one. They can tell you their opinion or give you tools to help direct your life in a positive way, but only God, Christ, and the Holy Spirit can fully transform you to what you're meant to be. If we aren't actively working toward living how God wants us to live, both inwardly and outwardly, we could stay complacent and not growing in Christ, never reaching our full potential.

Humankind brought original sin into this world. "You do you" is something I hear a lot. God's word, which is throughout the Old and New Testament, is the word and the truth. As most Christians understand, we know He is the truth, but it's so easy to get caught up listening to other people that we drift and think "you do you" is okay and accepted. What if the "you do you" happens to be criticizing and judging everyone? Is that okay? What if the "you do you" is bullying and belittling people or being promiscuous and having sex with whomever? You do you, right? We've come to accept any and all behavior because we're doing what we think we should do. We don't want to offend anyone by saying otherwise, or we are scared to stand up for the truth because it could cost us everything. I often ask myself, Is "me being me" a good thing?—me, someone born already having sin within me; me, someone who is quick to anger when I'm or someone else I know is disrespected; me, someone who will put you in your place if you are disrespectful; me, someone who has an ego and is selfish; me, someone who is only doing what's best for myself and family, not caring about anything or anybody else. Or should I be the "me" God wants me to be, the one who knows my heart, the one that doesn't rely on my own understanding but instead asks God what to do, who strives to be selfless, someone who will bend over backward to help if you're in need and not put my own needs first, someone who is humble and tries to be slow to anger, someone who is loyal and kind, someone who offers grace to everyone?

Now let me circle back around. If you had a choice, would you want to be around the "you do you" part of me or the me God wants me to be? We all have a choice, and it's up to us to make it. We verbally can say we believe in God, but our actions and what we do with our time can prove otherwise. When you live in faith and trust within the Holy Spirit is when blessings will happen. You will truly be alive, not just living. A new *you* will happen! I'm going to be completely honest; if you're reading this and have been feeling, deep down, something is missing, that you aren't truly happy deep within your soul, or you're having to take different things to make it through life, your faith is probably on yourself and your reputation. When my faith was on myself, I probably drank too much. I was mad and had resentment toward people that treated me poorly. I had no patience. I gossiped way too much, and I cared too much about what others thought. It happened so easily and without me knowing. I had this perception that my heart wouldn't deceive me. It's amazing how the devil can mentally keep you trapped, thinking you can do it all on your own while being so lonely on the inside. Look at Eve and how subtle the serpent was.

> But the serpent said to the woman, "You will not die. For God knows that when you eat of it your eyes will be opened, and you will be like God, knowing good and evil." (Genesis 3:4–5)

The serpent used God's own words to convince her to turn away from knowing only good to accepting evil into her life and continuing on with life on her own, the majority of the time we will miss when the serpent is staring us right in the face and telling us lies, things like I will never get out of this addiction, I will never be good enough, I will never get out of this depression, I will never stop having anxiety, I will never be pretty or skinny enough, I will never be happy while living, so I should just take my life. Until you put your faith in God and let Him renew your mind, you may find yourself always battling your inner thoughts that keep you trapped. Like I said before, who we watch or follow is so important. Protecting your mind is top priority. It all starts there. Until I knew who God was and how to rebuke evil, I had to be careful who I hung around with and what I watched. One crucial thing for me was who I followed on social media. My void was shopping, and most of who I followed were fashion influencers—not a good combination when you're realizing you shop to fill a void. I had to delete a lot of accounts and instead found myself following people that would help me on my spiritual journey. As my life changed, so did the people I followed. I still have my passion for fashion and beauty; it's just not at the top of my priority list. I can't say this enough: who and what you follow matter.

The Importance of Prayer

All my life I believed in God, but still I relied on myself. Before Bible study, I only prayed to God when something bad was going on in my life or when it was convenient for me. I never thanked or praised Him for what He had already given me. I was selfish. I didn't know what it was like to have a relationship with God. I didn't know how to pray until I fully started to understand the Bible. It eventually became a big part of my life. I started to find an immense amount of peace and clarity every time I prayed, so I continued day after day. I just felt better and more relaxed, which I think resulted in decreased anxiety. He already knows the outcome, so I'm casting all my burdens onto Him.

> Come to me, all of you who are tired
> from carrying heavy loads, and I will give
> you rest. (Matthew 11:28)

I had to learn the importance of prioritizing my prayer life.

> And whatever you ask in prayer, you will receive, if you have Faith. (Matthew 21:22)

The more my faith grew, the more I prayed. I could see and was experiencing how my life was night and day from two years prior, and I didn't want it to stop. Last year, November 2021, I wrote down multiple prayers I had been praying for. It wasn't to hold God accountable for answering my prayers but to look back and see if any of them had been answered. I don't know about you, but some nights I'm so tired that I forget what I prayed for by the time I wake up the next morning. It's life and reality; I guess. But I wanted a way to track it so I wouldn't miss the opportunity to thank Him if one was answered. One prayer in particular that I wrote down was for God to introduce new ladies into my life, ones that would help me grow in my faith and accept me for me. Up to this point, I was on this journey by myself. My friends still loved and accepted me for the path I was taking but didn't truly understanding the impact God was having on my life. I don't think even my parents or siblings knew. To be honest, I didn't want them or the world to know. What was happening at that time was between me and God. I think it needed to stay that way until God was ready for me to talk.

I know God will put people in your life for a purpose, whether it's to help you grow, help you get through a bad time, or help you walk with Christ again. Whatever the reason, He will sometimes speak to you through someone. In January 2021, one Sunday before class began, a new teacher introduced herself. She was starting halfway through the year, but I welcomed the new face because she had a calmness about her. Her aura was comforting to be around. I was new to teaching, a little over three months to be exact. I was still trying to find my groove with being a Sunday school teacher, and to have her next door to my room put me at ease. We became friends, but it stayed at church for a long time. Let's remember, I had quit blogging three months earlier, and Bible study and prayers were nonexistent at that point. I was fresh out of being a hot mess. It wasn't that I was hiding; I was just still confused as to where my life was heading. I knew God had just arrived on the scene and had a lot of work to do. I was still trying to learn how to listen to Him and adjust my life to living His way, not mine. I wasn't ready to let anyone new in yet until it was time.

Fast-forward a few months to November 2021, with the new school year upon us, the second year of us teaching together, I was halfway through with Bible study and was starting to experience what walking with Christ truly felt like. I had an active prayer life at this point and wrote on that prayer list for God to send women into my life that would help me grow in my faith. At this point, I didn't want to go back to my old habits. I had no idea what would come of that prayer, but it was important to me, so I wrote it down in my journal. Days turned into weeks; the busyness of life was carrying on as usual. It's sad to say, I forgot about writing down that prayer because once it was a few pages back in my journal, it was out of sight and out of mind. Life was good though; I was still walking on this new path of life and having so much gratitude for how far I've come in just a few short years.

In January 2022, I was asked by my friend at church, who I taught with, if I would be interested in helping to start a family ministry within our church. Without second-guessing, I immediately said yes. There were no hesitations because I knew I just went through a profound experience over the last year and a half that was life-changing. I had a deep desire to help other people experience that same thing too. Sometimes all it takes is walking through the front door for God to change your life.

Not knowing what exactly the other ladies had in mind, I showed up at our first breakfast meeting to discuss thoughts and opinions on how to make our church more family friendly and how to help welcome the families who may have drifted. That morning, I met the lady behind the vision, Kristen. Her personality can't be matched. She's energetic, passionate, loving, and would literally give you the shirt off her back if you needed it. She gives so much to others, not expecting anything in return. She had this desire to bring people back to the church and wanted help orchestrating it. We sat at that restaurant for hours, sharing our thoughts and getting to know each other. By the end of the meeting, we learned we all shared one common goal: We wanted more fellowship within our church; we wanted our kids to enjoy coming, and we wanted families to feel like they belonged in that parish. After planning our first event and getting it approved by our priest, the Faith and Family Fellowship Ministry was created. Two years ago, I was lost, but now I am found and starting a ministry—another "who would have ever thought" moment! I think it surprised my family when I told them too. To say I've come full circle is an understatement. As we planned monthly events, we became closer and closer. These ladies, who I barely knew, were turning into dear friends of mine. It seemed like I'd known some of them my whole life, but we just met six months prior. To develop this kind of friendship so fast as an adult is pretty amazing. One weekend, I happened to pull out my journal in which I wrote down my prayers dated from November 2021. On that list were five or six prayers, one in which was that prayer where I was asking God to bring women into my life that would help me grow in my faith. Boy, did He answer that prayer, and He answered it without me realizing it.

Remember that Sunday school teacher who started halfway through my first year of teaching back in 2020, the one whose aura was comforting to me? Well, her name is Lu, and Lu originally wasn't supposed to move here. She originally was buying a hundred-year-old fixer upper house on the complete other side of town, but something unexpectedly came up with her husband's job and, one random day, after getting stuck in traffic, rerouted them to pass through my town. My little town in South Carolina, the town they ended up moving to. Also, unexpectedly, the current second-grade Sunday school teacher left halfway through that same year and around that same time. Guess who volunteered to take that position? Lu. Lu met Kristen because she taught her son at church. Kristen had the desire to get a group of women together and start a ministry. Lu reached out to me and invited me to join. I know, in my heart, this wasn't a coincidence. I know God had a hand in bringing us all together. Within this group of ladies, we share and help each other get through struggles we face. We laugh together. We pray together and will go through a new year of Bible study together. I am forever grateful for God for placing Lu on my path to open a door to meet ladies and bond on such a spiritual level.

> If you abide in me, and my words
> abide in you, ask whatever you will, and it
> shall be done for you. (John 15:7)

This is 100 percent true because I've experienced it first-hand. If walking with Christ and leading a life for Him can transform me, He can transform you too. Sometimes God can do the most work when you're suffering and, through that suffering, bring you closer to Him, living a life in like-ness of Him. He knows what we go through because He's experienced suffering Himself. When He sent Jesus to walk this earth in human form, He got to experience what we experience. He got to experience what battling evil looks and feels like. He got to experience the same temptations we battle today. He knows what we're going through when we're dealing with suffering. He doesn't leave us to figure it out on our own. He's actually there, walking by your side; we just need to let Him in, just like Christ had to suffer before having His redemption in heaven. Sometimes we have to suffer to find our redemption through Jesus Christ. Through our suffering and redemption, a fire that lives within us becomes alive and can awaken us to fight a battle that's bigger than our own, the battle of good versus evil.

> Finally, be strong in the Lord and in the strength of his might. Put on the whole armor of God, that you may be able to stand against the wiles of the devil. For we are not contending against flesh and blood, but against the principalities, against the powers, against the world rulers of this present darkness, against the spiritual hosts of wickedness in the heavenly places. Therefore take the whole armor of God, that you may be able to withstand in the evil day, and having done all, to stand. (Ephesians 6: 10–13)

Finding My Redemption

A s we all are aware, no one is exempt from evil. No matter your age or ethnicity, we are all subject to bad things happening. Whether we create the bad thing or are on the receiving end, we will all experience it at some point in our life. Looking at the world around me, our culture, idolizing other idols, and the rise in mental illness and suicide among all ages are alarming and very concerning to me. According to NPR, suicide is the second leading cause of death in kids ages five through eleven years old. In adults, eighteen years and older, there is one suicide death every eleven minutes, according to the CDC. Let that sink in.

Every time I turned on the news (which I don't watch anymore), I felt an overwhelming concern for my daughters and the world they would grow up in. Learning to trust Him can be scary because our culture teaches us to solely rely on ourselves. We've taken God out of school completely. We've forgotten (myself included, for a number of years) how to pray and really hear God's voice. We, as a society, have become very selfish. And instead of serving, we are waiting to be served. Evil is sneaky.

> Be sober, be watchful. Your adversary
> the devil prowls around like a roaring lion,
> seeking someone to devour. (1 Peter 5:8)

The devil is smart. Look how he influenced Adam and Eve in the garden of Eden. If we are constantly on social media, following and watching the wrong people, the devil has a straight portal into our soul and minds. Once it finds your vice, it will lay into it until it succeeds. It found mine. Again, with God being taken out of everything, how are we to fight against it? Our culture and norm are to pop a pill. That would have been the easy way out for me. It would be way easier for me to mask the problem with medication versus taking a hard look at myself and how I'm living my life. Change is hard and scary; I get it. I've lived it. If you're like me where you know, deep down, something needs to change but aren't sure which way to go, take a breath and take that first step by asking God to lead. You'll still feel lost on what to do; I sure did. Heck, I still feel lost some days, but I had to learn to let go of the what ifs and the control for the future and start living for today. God knows my future, and I know He will lead me through it on His time. If I chose to take medicine to mask my underlying problems two years prior, would I have experienced the same thing? Would I still be stuck listening to a lie that tells me that these are all life has to offer: stress and anxiety? Honestly, I'm not sure. But what I am sure of is, as long as we are breathing, the devil will be trying to attack us in any way, shape, or form. He doesn't get the last word. Don't let Him have the last word. Like I tell my girls when negative thoughts enter their mind, "Not today. You don't get to mess with me." When you're facing difficult challenges and deciding what path to take on your journey, you get to choose who to listen to. Just remember, when choosing, God will always win and will have the last word. He made that clear when He created Jesus Christ.

> Let us know, let us press on to know
> the Lord; his going forth is sure as the
> dawn; he will come to us as the showers,
> as the spring rains that water the earth.
> (Hosea 6:3)

A little background on Hosea. He was a prophet in the Old Testament. The people in Israel at that time were faithless and had no knowledge of God. They were killing, stealing, and living in sin. The Lord knew He was sending a savior and used Hosea to preach to the people. He needed them to repent and turn toward God again. God knew he was more powerful than the evil that occupied the present world, and He knew He would have the final say. His assurance to us to send a savior was as sure as dawn coming every evening. With that savior, a new life would happen, like a spring rain that brings new life to earth. Whatever you're facing, don't give up. Press on through your mistakes and pain while staying focused on God, providing and seeing you through. He will, if you let Him.

I don't know if I made a mistake starting Meganmariestyles, and God is using it for the greater good, or if I was supposed to go through that experience so I could be of great ministry for Him. Maybe I was supposed to be an influencer, just one of a different kind. I know what social media can do to a person; I know what influencers are going through. I can relate on a level most people or parents can't. God knew my heart and was strong enough to bring me out on the other side to help minister to people going through the same thing. I know what I experienced is deeper than I will ever realize or imagine. God gave me my personality, my loudness, my directness, my passion for things I love, and some would say my quirkiness for a reason, and I'm trusting Him to use it for the greater good. Who knew He would actually be listening while I was driving my car or use my child to speak to me because I'm too hardheaded to listen to anyone else. All you have to do is ask. When you consistently seek Him, and I'm not talking about just on Sunday. I'm talking about actively, every day; growing in His knowledge is when you will receive what's graciously been given to us. Your door will be opened. It may not be right away. It's on His time, and that may look a lot different than ours, but you'll get there. And once you're there, it will make life so much sweeter. Personally, I had to learn to listen to that inner voice: the spirit of God. Once I did, it was a game changer. I will never go back. I don't want to go back to my "normal" life. I'm not exempt from bad things happening. There will still be good days and bad days, that's life. How I handle and walk through them is the difference. I know, no matter how bad things get, there is someone who exceeds all power walking with me through it. That's the difference.

> But you are a chosen race, a royal priesthood, a holy nation, God's own people, that you may declare the wonderful deeds of him who called you out of darkness into his marvelous light. (1 Peter 1:9)

If He chose me, He is choosing you too!

Following My Purpose

Hope has two beautiful daughters; their names are anger and courage, anger at the way things are, and courage to see that they do not remain as they are.

—Saint Augustine

I started to have this urge to help people. I could see people hurting and struggling and wanted to show them there's another way. I wanted to help them experience the love from God, the same love I've experienced. You don't have to turn to pills to numb the pain. You don't have to develop an addiction to a substance to manage life. You don't have to show your body off or have sex with random people to feel loved. You don't have to physically hurt yourself to get out of pain. I'm so tired of seeing evil win. I had to do something, but what or how?

After attending a Bible study meeting, I went home, still thinking I had a deeper purpose. I prayed that day, asking God to show me what I was supposed to do next. What was my purpose? I knew it was more than what I was already doing. That night I woke up wide awake around 3:00 a.m. from a dead sleep and had an overwhelming feeling to write a book, to tell my story. I couldn't go back to sleep because I was trying to decipher if I had been dreaming or if God was trying to tell me something. I woke my husband up in the early morning hours to relay all my thoughts on what happened the night before and to get his opinion. I sat quietly after I finished telling him to see what his thoughts were. I didn't know if he would look at me like I was crazy or if he would understand because he's been a witness and experiencing my journey over the last two years. He's been there for the good, the bad, and the ugly. He's been there to witness me accepting Jesus Christ in my life. He's been there to see a change not only within me but our entire family. His reaction could go either way.

As I looked on waiting for him to fully wake up to comprehend what I just said, he simply said, "Yes, I think that would be a good thing. You're good with relating to people, and I think it could help someone." Wait, what? Reality was hitting that I'd be vulnerable. I'd be exposed putting something so personal out there for the world to see. Him saying, "no, you're crazy" would be my reason as to why I wouldn't listen to that voice telling me to write a book and confirming the voice telling me to stay in my bubble. It would be safer that way. I battled this thought in my mind for a couple days, night after night praying and sleeping on it. It ultimately went back to, like it always does, the promise I gave two years prior. I would listen and trust. So that's what I did; I started writing my story. This book is for my two beautiful daughters. This book is for anyone struggling with anxiety or depression and being stuck in a mental stronghold. This book is for young kids getting on social media. This book is for young adults trying to find their self-worth and self-esteem. This book is for moms and dads trying to do it all by themselves and feeling like they have to be perfect while doing so. This book is for anyone holding on to shame for their sins. This book is about me finding my redemption through Jesus Christ. This book is about me following my purpose.

In *February 2020*, in the midst of blogging and living a selfish life, I told God I needed Him and would listen. The next day, I walked away from blogging. *May 2020*, I volunteered to become a Sunday school teacher. *December 2020*, I was leaving my place of employment, not having anything else lined up, just knowing in my heart I needed to. *January 2021*, Lu walked into my life and volunteered to become a Sunday school teacher. *March 2021*, Dr. Lopez with Gaston Perio Office fell into my lap, and I started making money, filling in at their amazing office. *September 2021*, I started my first Bible study. *January 2022*, Lu reached out because Kristen wanted to start a ministry and needed help. *March 2022*, Faith and Family Fellowship Ministry was born. *October 2022*, I was telling my story. If you let God renew your mind, He can do some amazing things.

I wrote down this timeline because you can clearly see God's hand in my life. I didn't notice or realize it on a daily basis. Some days I felt like He couldn't or wouldn't hear me, but looking back, He was clearly hearing something I was saying. My advice to you: Don't get discouraged or give up if you're going through something, and it's not changing right away. We have to be open in realizing that what He's preparing for us may not look like what we envisioned. Explore your spiritual strengths or your charisms. God gives them to all of us. Exploring them and finding the ones God gave personally to you will help you find your purpose. Staying true to that gift and His word will get you to your purpose. Once you know your purpose, no matter how big or small, put action to it. Whatever action it is could be a stepping stone for what's next in your life. Let Him bring you out of your own mind, your own Egypt, and your own slavery that's holding you back from your promised land. Let Him give you heaven on earth. I would have never believed it if you would have told me in February 2020, I would be living my life this way or would be a part of starting a ministry and now writing a book. It's absolutely amazing. I'm so glad God gave me the courage to follow with faith and let Him lead. My personality He put in me, that I was born with, was for a reason. My fierce competitiveness and drive that has been present since I was a little girl is starting to make sense. Do I think I'm where He wants me to be? No, He's not done with me, He's just getting started.

Finding Hope when
It's Hard to See

◆

So that through two unchangeable things, in which it
is impossible that God should prove false, we who have
fled from refuge might have strong encouragement
to seize the hope set before us. We have this as a
sure and steadfast anchor of the soul, a hope that
enters into the inner shrine behind the curtain.

—Hebrews 6:18–19

The two unchangeable things are the promise and oath.
God promised a hope that would be found through
Christ.

We normally think hope represents something we
wish for, like I hope you have a great day. It's not a guarantee we're going to have a great day, but we can wish we
have a great day. In the Bible and in biblical terms, hope is
described as something steadfast and a sure anchor to our
soul. So when the verse tells us we have a hope that enters
into the inner shrine behind the curtain, it's not a wish. It's

a promise that when we take refuge within God, we will have a hope placed in our soul that is sure and steadfast.

No one knows who wrote the book of Hebrews, but it describes how important Jesus Christ is and where He ranks, higher than the angels. He intercedes for us and is able through the Spirit to reach places that are hidden deep within our soul, something that could not be done in the Old Testament.

> Where Jesus has gone as a forerunner on our behalf, having become a high priest for ever after the order of Melchizedek. (Melchizedek means you are a king and a priest). (Hebrews 6:20)

Hebrews, chapter 6, verses 18 through 20, shows how important it is to never give up and to grow in our faith. It's a promise of hope that Jesus gives to us through the Spirit that allows Him to look at our innermost self, the damaged part, the part that needs to be saved, and the part that needs to take refuge. It's a promise of God's word and oath in which Jesus laid the path for us to have a steadfast anchor of our soul. It's the hope that lives deep within us. If you allow Him, He can give you your life back. Yes, we will get lost sometimes. Yes, we will sin. Yes, we will battle evil most days of our lives. Yes, we will go through chaos, wondering where God is in our life. Just because a situation doesn't make sense right now and we don't understand doesn't mean He wants us to give up. Keep going. Keep the faith, praying through the hard times and thanking Him through the good. Have *hope* that tomorrow will be a better day because Jesus paved a path for you. Don't let evil win. Have courage to be the you God made you to be. Remember, He chose *you*!

The Silent Speaker

It's been six months since I've started writing my testimony and the questions I have surrounding who controls our innermost self and whose voice dictates how we feel with ourselves and the people in our lives. Who controls this voice, and who has the power to change it? Is it God, the devil, ourself as an individual, or do we have no control, something we're just born with? What voice is making people stay stuck in addiction, and what voice makes people thrive to live their best life? What made my inner voice be the exact opposite of my outer voice during my blogging days? My personal answer to who the silent speaker is, it's all three: me, God, and the devil/evil. Through research and studying the Bible, I think I found my answer, and it comes from two scripture verses.

> You are of your father the devil, and your will is to do your father's desires. He was a murderer from the beginning, and has nothing to do with the truth, because there is no truth in him. When he lies, he speaks according to his own nature, for he is a liar and the father of lies. (John 8:44)

For the word of God is living and active, sharper than any two-edged sword, piercing to the division of soul and spirit, of joints and marrow, and discerning the thoughts and intentions of the hearts. (Hebrews 4:12)

I would highly recommend reading John, chapter 8, in its entirety. To give you the cliff notes, Jesus saw the Jewish people believing the way they lived their life was acceptable to God because they were Abraham's descendants. They thought, since Abraham was from God, and they were from Abraham, that automatically made them children of God. They've never been physically in bondage to anyone, so why would they need to be set free? They had a hard time believing Jesus was the Son of God sent to set them free from their sins because they were so accustomed to the high priest, offering sacrifices on their behalf. I would imagine pride and power took over some of their hearts and got in the way of them seeing Jesus as the Son of God. Since we knew the ending and they were living it in real time, I try to put myself in their shoes. Would I have believed He was the Son of God? If I had kings and priests telling me this guy named Jesus was spreading lies and not to be trusted, would I have listened to them or followed my heart? His own disciples had a hard time with following theirs, especially when Peter denied Jesus three times. Would I have believed those high priests had my best interest at heart versus their own desires for power? If you think about it, we're living in the same times. Instead of kings in charge, we have presidents and prime ministers. Most of us are living our life with what we think is acceptable to God because we're baptized and Christians, but are we truly living how God wants us to live?—just food for thought.

Back to the scripture from John and Jesus educating the Jewish people on who their father was...

The verse from above (John 8:44) is Jesus telling the Jewish people who their original father was, the devil, brought into the world by the first original sin, and our will is to do our father's desires. He speaks according to his own nature and knows no truth. He is the father of lies. Could that be why we have one inner voice telling us we aren't good enough; we'll never succeed; or to succeed, we need to lie and destroy until we have all the power? That inner voice telling us we'll never be happy, so why bother? That inner voice that keeps us stuck with lies? Was Jesus trying to tell the Jewish people He was sent from God to set them free from the innermost part of their soul, stemming from the first original sins and their own—something only His blood could do because God is stronger and more powerful than the devil, something that Melchizedek or any high priest could never fully accomplish with the sacrificial offerings of animals from the Old Testament?

Moving along to the letter to the Hebrews, knowing who our original father is...

> For the word of God is living and
> active, sharper than any two-edged sword,
> piercing to the division of soul and spirit,
> of joints and marrow, and discerning the

thoughts and intentions of the hearts. (Hebrews 4:12)

Is God the second inner voice, battling the first (our original father), a voice so powerful that it's sharper than any two-edged sword and can pierce the division of the soul and spirit and bring them back together? Could this be how God is the most powerful and will always win against evil, but it's our choice to make, which voice we listen to, or which path we take? Could this be where the innermost voices that control our lives come from? Could this be why it's so important to walk with God because it helps to silence the voice stemming from our original father? I know, in my heart, this explains the division between my two voices within myself. When I was blogging, focusing only on my family, myself, and living for materialist things to make me happy, I had an inner voice that told me that I wasn't enough and would never be enough among other things. A dark and lonely place. When I turned my life over to God and started listening to Him and His truth, that is when that inner voice started to change. Every day, I woke up and chose to focus and listen to Him. Was my life perfect? Absolutely not. Did I still struggle with sin? Yes. Listening to God's voice brought my soul and spirit together. I had light in my life and in my soul. My inner voice finally matched my outer voice. That was the difference. I understand that now.

I would encourage you to reread and think about those two verses for a minute and relate them to your life—not the life everyone sees, the outer voice, but the life that lives within you, behind the curtain, the inner voice only you see and hear. Which one is controlling that hidden voice for you? Now look at our world and the mental state of people around you? Knowing who our original father is, the one that lies, could that be why suicide is a leading cause of death in the United States (according to the CDC)? Could that be why there are so many people addicted to substances or pornography, trying to feel good for a moment in time, knowing it won't last? Have we listened to that negative voice for so long that we've forgotten the voice that holds the truth and the most power? That negative inner voice doesn't have to stay. We have a choice, and it's up to us to make. It's up to us, as individuals, to pursue Jesus, to let Him have our whole heart and live by His word. When you fully commit to God is when our original father, the devil, will know he's not in charge anymore and will come knocking full force.

> Put on the whole armor of God, that you may be able to stand against the wiles of the devil. (Ephesians 6:11)

Are you ready?

Social Media Side Effects

I think it's very important to make parents aware of some things I saw and experienced while blogging. Looking back, I'm so thankful I went through this experience because it prepared me to better help educate my daughters, young adults, and parents on some of the hidden dangers with social media accounts. Hands down if you can prolong your child from having social media accounts (YouTube included); do it. Let them stay kids as long as possible. If your child already has accounts set up, and you see them becoming addicted or see them struggling with depression or anxiety, have them take a break from all social media platforms. I would encourage parents to do the same.

As adults, we can get distracted just as easily as our children. We can become addicted ourselves. Taking a mental break and focusing on who you are as a person is healthy. Start by taking a week off; it will be hard because it's amazing how addicting scrolling through random posts can be. For me personally, I had to download a daily Bible verse app and Solitaire. They were placed front and center of my phone's home page. Instead of immediately checking Instagram or Facebook first thing in the morning like I used to, I would instead read a Bible scripture or play a quick game of solitaire. Keep the faith. If I can undo my addiction, you or your child can too. Remember, you're the parent! I can guarantee, your teenager may struggle and not like you for the first few days when taking their social media away, but it will be short-lived compared to the long-term benefits he or she will have.

Before allowing your child back on social media evaluate their self-esteem or confidence within themselves. A lot of children are too young to fully understand their self-worth through God's eyes. They may only know their self-worth through likes or comments from other people. If they are judging their happiness or acceptance through pictures they post on social media, that is a red flag. If they compare their life to someone else's, it will only get worse when they go online. It could make them feel not good enough. They may not know that the picture they're looking at could have been photoshopped and isn't truly real. Things are not always as they appear. When they're in middle or high school, there will be times when their friends are invited to places they aren't, and that can lead to feeling of depression, when in reality, God may not want those people in their life to begin with. What you see on any social media site is never true reality. What God created in you is only for you, no one else. If we constantly compare our lives to someone else's, we may miss out on the gifts we were given and His purpose He puts within us.

> The purpose in a man's mind is like
> deep water, but a man of understanding
> will draw it out. (Proverbs 20:5)

The more we read scripture and understand God's word, the more we can understand our purpose. If we never truly understand God's word, our purpose will stay buried in the deep water. Don't let scrolling through someone else's feed affect your happiness or compromise your purpose.

Red Flags

I was very naive when I started out on social media. I don't think I fully understood how, if it is used in the wrong way or at too earlier of an age, it could impact one's mental health. Protecting our minds is so important. We have to make sure we educate our kids on a number of things in life to keep them and others safe. Social media is one of those things.

1) *Body image*—It can affect both girls and boys. It's not reality for every guy to have muscles protruding out of their bodies and girls to be stick thin with thigh gaps. Yes, there are some, but it's not the majority. Body image is a huge concern for people of all ages. When you scroll through countless photos of other people on different apps, and you're constantly comparing your body to theirs, it will become a problem. If a young adult is already struggling with body image among his or her peers, it will only get worse if they get online and start comparing themselves to thousands of other people. A large percentage of photos on these sites are altered to some degree, whether it's a filter to make your face look brighter, smoother, less wrin-

kled, or to slim a part of your body down that you may not like. We alter photos to make ourselves look more attractive online, therefore it makes us feel better in real life. I'm not saying all photos are being altered, but a lot are. I'm also not saying it's necessarily a bad thing because I've done it a few times when I needed a certain look for a photo. It does warrant a discussion as to why we think we need to alter a photo of ourselves and whether it is healthy to create made-up images of how we're supposed to look. There are hundreds of body-contouring apps readily available on any phone, and most of the time they're free to download. If we thought self-image was a problem with body modifications they made on magazine covers years ago, social media sites took it to a whole new level. Comparison will rob you of your true worth. This leads me to my next precaution.

2) *Self-worth*—Not knowing your self-worth can be detrimental to your mental health. Self-worth doesn't come from affirmations from friends on what you look like. It doesn't come from how many likes you get on a picture or video online. And it doesn't come from a spouse or partner. It comes from God. He created us in likeness of Him. We are beautiful and perfect, no matter our skin color, shape, or size. Until we know and understand that, at our core, we are at risk of falling into a cycle where we base our happiness, our self-worth on the feedback and attention we get from other people.

3) *Gossip*—Social media can be a direct portal to gossip. There are so many Bible verses speaking about gossip and the damage it can cause. It's a betrayal of confidence and can ruin many relationships. If you hear yourself or your child talking about someone or something they saw posted on a social media site, at school, or at someone else's house, ask yourself if it could be considered slander. Gossip can influence a gang-like mentality and possibly draw good people into bad situations. It takes one person to spread false lies to others, which can ruin a person's reputation. It's always been a problem in friend groups but is magnified online. Think about if that person is you or your child. A lot of times, most negative articles written about a particular person or group is meant to maliciously hurt someone because the author doesn't agree with their way of thinking. It's only done to bully an individual, make money, or get attention. A lot of times, it's not based on facts, just their opinions.

Look at how much magazines and other online sites get paid to write about other people. For some reason we love to gossip, as long as it's not about ourselves. School-age kids who are on the receiving end of gossip from other kids in their class can experience a decline in their self-esteem and self-worth. We all remember middle school. It's hard. Hormones are raging, we're growing and changing, and we're all trying to figure out who we are because we aren't little kids anymore. It's a confusing time, but we all figure it out at some point. Gossip is something we overlook and we don't think is harmful because it's not actually bullying. We don't take into account what that person is battling internally or in their personal life. I'm not exempt from this. I used to gossip way too much until I actually thought about how my words spoken to other people could be hurting the person I was talking about. It's something that I still struggle with. When I hear someone gossiping, it's so easy to jump back on that train. Learning to walk away or not involve myself in responding will usually help shut it down and change the subject.

> A fool's lips bring strife, and his mouth invites a flogging. A fool's mouth is his ruin and his lips are a snare to himself. (Proverbs 18:7–8)

> He who keeps his mouth and his tongue keeps himself out or trouble. (Proverbs 21:23)

4) *Being left out*—Kids notice who's hanging out with whom, who's being invited to certain parties or gatherings. Kids can be left feeling like they don't belong or don't fit in. If they are having a hard time finding their group at school, it will be even harder for them watching other groups hang out online. Just because they weren't invited to a party, sleepover, or gathering doesn't mean they're less than. It doesn't mean they're not cool enough, or they're

not wanted. It simply means those groups may not be the best people to hang out with, and that's okay, or they don't know how awesome you are! This is a hard one for me coming from the standpoint of a mom. I tell my girls this all the time, but it doesn't mean my heart hurts any less for them.

5) *Bullies*—Bullies aren't just at school anymore. They can have direct access to you or your child. They can post and say hateful things about anyone and anything when they're behind a keyboard. Some of them are bots (fake accounts) designed to start arguments and to hurt people. When a child is getting bullied online, and they already have feelings like they don't belong, with negative thoughts entering their brain, it can lead to very negative consequences. Unfortunately, no age is exempt from evil.

6) *Sexual advances*—This one I didn't expect, but it happens more often than not. It makes me very concerned since I have two daughters. It doesn't matter if you're male or female; it can happen at any age and to any gender. I've personally experienced inappropriate comments and older men asking me if I needed a sugar daddy and how much they would pay me weekly. Other than reading them to my husband and thinking grossly, I didn't pay attention to those messages and quickly deleted them. However, a young child may not know the dangers behind it. I think of a vulnerable young girl who may not have the best male figure in her life and is subconsciously searching for someone to fill that void (whether she knows it or not) or show

her love. How easy it could be for her to fall into that trap of possibly being sexually exploited. On the other hand, convince these young kids to take pictures of themselves, then use them as pawns to demand whatever they want. Sexual harassment happens on social media and is something we need to pay attention to and educate our kids on.

7) *Being influenced by the wrong people*—Who we follow matters. Who we hang out with matters. Have you ever heard the saying that if you lay down with dogs, you get fleas? Well, if you follow the wrong people, you will eventually start to act like them. If your child follows people that glamourize showing off their bodies, your child could soon start doing the same. If they follow people who think having multiple sex partners is a cool thing, your child could soon be sexually active. If you have an addiction to food and follow a lot of cooking influencers, you're probably going to have a hard time losing weight and getting healthy. If you follow or watch people who spread hate on a particular party or group, you're probably going to start to have the same kind of hate in your heart. *Who we watch and follow matters!* This is so important, and that's why I saved it for last. This one doesn't just relate to young kids; this affects all adults too, myself included. What we watch determines what we think about. It starts mentally in your mind. I can't say this enough: Pick who you watch, and follow carefully. Unfortunately, the news is not exempt from this.

God's Creation

G od created every one of us in His likeness. Let your self-worth come from Him and no one else. Our value isn't determined by the house we live in, the clothes we wear, how many friends we have, or how many compliments we get from other people. Our value and purpose come straight from God. It's our job, as parents, to help teach our children that. If we try to let our culture teach them their self-worth, it may be short-lived and will eventually fail. True acceptance and self-esteem come only from God and no other false idols. Below are a few verses I personally use to teach my daughters to know their value here on this earth. Once we talk about the verses, it opens up a conversation on how they feel about themselves. I do this weekly while driving them to school. I simply ask them to name a few things they love about themselves, things that God gave them. At first it was hard, and they didn't know what to say. I would go first to give them examples, but it made them really think, at a young age, about what God put in them that makes them special, what makes them unique, and what makes them beautiful. As they grow older and look at themselves in the mirror, my hope is that their inner self will see all the beautiful things God gave them and pick out the ones they love the most. No matter your shape, size, or skin color, we are all created in His likeness. We are all made beautiful.

> For she is a reflection of eternal light, a spotless mirror of the workings of God, and an image of his goodness. (Wisdom of Solomon 7:26)

> Do not be conformed to this world but be transformed by the renewal of your mind, that you may prove what is the will of God, what is good and acceptable and perfect. (Romans 12:2)

> For thou didst form my inward parts, thou didst knit me together in my mother's womb. I praise thee, for thou art fearful and wonderful. Wonderful are thy works! Thou knowest me right well; my frame was not hidden from thee, when I was being made in secret, intricately wrought in the depths of the earth. (Psalm 139:13–15)

> Are not five sparrows sold for two pennies? And not one of them is forgotten before God. Why, even the hairs of your head are numbered. Fear not; you are of

more value than many sparrows. (Luke 12:6–7)

For I know the plans I have for you, says the Lord, plans of welfare and not for evil, to give you a future and a hope. (Jeremiah 29:11)

Verse Study

I found I can't read the Bible as a normal book. I've tried and never succeeded. To really understand what God's word is, I have to take a few verses and really break it down. I think about the verse and ask myself questions: What is it saying? What does it mean to me? Can I apply it to anywhere in my life I need help? Can I identify with that verse in areas of my life that need to be evaluated? I write down all these questions and just sit in total silence, examining myself and life. Sometimes I would meditate and pray for God to help me understand what he's saying. Other times it was taking a hard look at myself and areas of my life I needed to involve God more in. It was a game changer with understanding the Bible and having happiness and love live within me. Like myself, so many people think happiness comes from an outside force. There's even a book about people's personalities and what they need to feel love from a partner, whether it's gifts, acts of service, verbal confirmation. I could go on with listing different affirmations. I'm not saying whoever wrote that book is wrong. What I am saying is, it will be short-lived. It will make you feel good in the moment when whatever affirmation fits you is happening, but it won't sustain you in the long run and within your soul. That can only be obtained when you have a relationship and live your life for Christ.

I never fully understood that until I started living my life for Him and reading His word in the Bible, not just reading scripture but fully understanding it. Until we realize and learn that our happiness comes from within, there will always be something missing, a void. These last two years, since our family started on this journey, my husband and I have seen a drastic improvement in our marriage, an improvement on how our daughters find their confidence, but most importantly we've seen a drastic improvement with our inner happiness. Life will never be perfect, but living a Christ-filled life can make walking through it on this earth a little better. It's right in the Lord's Prayer. Thy will be done on earth as it is in heaven. Without a shadow of a doubt, His way is so much better and so much sweeter. I can't take credit for figuring this out all on my own. The credit goes to walking with purpose and what that Bible study has taught me. I would encourage anyone, no matter your age, to sign up for one. It could change your life like it did mine.

I wanted to show you some examples of how I break down Bible verses to understand them and how I relate them to my own life. I've left some journaling space for you to write your thoughts with how it could relate to your life as well.

I am the vine, you are the branches.
He who abides in me, and I in him, he
it is that bears much fruit, for apart from

me you can do nothing. If a man does not abide in me, he is cast forth as a branch and withers; and the branches burned. If you abide in me, and my words abide in you, ask whatever you will, and it shall be done for you. By this my Father is glorified, that you bear much fruit, and so prove to be my disciples. As the Father has loved me, so have I loved you; abide in my love. (John 15:5–9)

1) Paraphrase it in your own words. Here is mine.

Jesus is the body. All things must come through Him, be by Him, and live within Him. If we are walking on His word and living by His word, we will be glorified on earth and receive many blessings. If we don't live in Christ and choose to walk in our own selfishness, we will wither away and not have a relationship with Him in our life. Everything starts and ends with Him. It's our choice to choose.

2) Relation to your life. Here is mine.

For me, personally, I love this verse. Two years ago, this verse didn't mean much, other than Jesus loves me. I was still lost and trying to do things on my own. I had anger and resentment for people who spoke and treated me poorly. I had so much anxiety, making life work in my favor. I had no clue what the cause was, but I knew taking a pill to deal with life and be happy wasn't an option for me. If I continued living life my way, I probably would eventually need medicine to help me control everything. I was cut off from Him. Once my life changed, I began to understand the root cause of my problem was not having a relationship with God and not abiding in Christ. I've been on both sides, and I can say, life was so much harder when I wasn't living life for Christ. When we're not living and putting Him first, we are cast forth as a branch and wither. Thrown into the fire and burned, we are cut off from His love and graces, leaving us to take a pill to feel happiness and less anxious. He is the vine, and I am the branch. I abide in Him and Him in me. I can only bear fruit through him. Apart from that, I can do nothing. It starts and ends with Christ. He will leave the ninety-nine to come find the one who got lost. He found me, and I know He will find you. We have a choice, and all we have to do is ask and obey. Believing in God and being a fan of His and living your life walking with Him are two totally different things.

A) Is there an area in your life that needs God's love and grace? Is there an area in your life leaving you feeling anxious or depressed? Have you also been told to take medicine to make yourself happy, or are you self-medicating with alcohol or another substance? Think about areas in your life, and see if you see God in it or yourself. Think about if you're walking in faith and letting God lead or if you're trying to control the outcome. Write it down, and pray for God to come into your life and relieve you of your preconceived notions as to how you should live your life. Ask Him for the courage to take action once He does find you. Ask Him to help you choose Him over any temptation in your life. Praise Him with gratitude and thank Him for loving you.

B) Are you the branch to His vine? What are some steps you can take to grow closer to God and learn to walk with Him?

I would encourage you to sit in silence and reflect on what you just wrote down. Ask God for His guidance in areas of your life that need help. I know life may seem hard, but we aren't meant to go through it alone. God knows who you are and wants you to have heaven on earth. Allow Him to show you the way. Allow Him to show you how to walk on faith and not sight.

Because God has made us for himself, our hearts are restless until they rest in him. (St. Augustine)

Communication Tip

I first want to say thank you if you read this book. Your support means the world to me. I originally wrote this book for my daughters, who are eight and ten years old. I wanted something to help them when they become pre-teen, teenagers, and young adults. You know, before they think they're smarter than everyone else. For kids, I feel reading or journaling can be a great way to communicate because they're going through so many changes that they may not know how to express what they're feeling or could be embarrassed to express how they really feel. To them, we're mom, who is exempt from any evil thing happening in the world, who has never experienced or had to deal with anything bad or embarrassing. So how could we understand? I remember, a few years ago, I was at a ladies' luncheon at my aunt's church. I started talking to a lady whose kids were in college and were close to getting married. I asked her if she had any advice for the teenage years, and her response was something I've never forgotten and started implementing right away. It was like a light bulb went off in my head. Why hadn't I thought of this? When her daughter was in high school, they had their own journal they shared between them. Her daughter could write whatever she wanted to, how she was feeling, or what she was going through at the time. It could be about anything. When she was done and ready to give it to her mom, she would lay it on her mom's bed. Her mom would write back and return it underneath the daughter's pillow. Whatever was written in the journal between the two was never discussed verbally unless the daughter wanted to. It kept an open line of communication. Whatever the daughter was going through, she didn't have to go through it alone.

I think having that kind of communication is critical to understanding what's going on inside your child's world and mind. With this ever-changing digital world, having them feel safe enough without embarrassment or judgment to come to you is a pretty awesome thing. I knew I wanted that kind of relationship and communication with my daughters, so I quickly picked up a journal and explained to my oldest how to use it. We've been writing back and forth for months. Yes, it's mainly minor things, but she's learning there is more than one way to communicate. Let's face it, when you become a teenager and have hormones racing through your body, any slight eye movement or facial expression can set off an argument and/or a slammed door or two. Sorry, Mom and Dad. Eventually, it could lead to them shutting you out completely and turning to others for advice. Having them share their life with you through a journal while they're growing, changing, and trying to figure it out can alleviate the mistaken facial expressions or tone of your voice, making them feel less judged or criticized and safe to share whatever they're going through (good or bad). I wanted to include this in case someone is having a hard time verbally communicating with their child. Being aware of what your child is experiencing could save their life.

Questions for Discussion

1. Discuss ways you see God in your life. Do you see areas in your life you're trying to control? Do you see areas He's already working?
2. If you are on social media, how do you feel when you log off? Does it make you feel less than? Does it inspire you?
3. When on social media, do you find yourself comparing your life to someone else?
4. Do you hold anger or resentment for a certain situation or person because of how they've treated you? Have you asked God for help?
5. Discuss ways God has enriched your life!
6. Discuss how you feel confident. Do you only feel confident when you're getting likes and positive comments from friends on social media or in person? Do you base your self-worth on those comments?
7. Explain all the beautiful qualities God put in you when He made you!
8. Does my behavior resemble selfishness, or would God be proud of me?

9. Discuss ways to improve prayer. How can you communicate with God on a daily basis?
10. Are you hanging around a crowd that keeps you stuck in a certain lifestyle? Do they hold you back from leading a Christlike life?
11. What are some ways I can walk with Christ?
12. Are there any areas in your town that need help? Discuss ways to volunteer.

Journaling Space

Journaling Space

Journaling Space

About the Author

M egan Ross, author of *The Silent Speaker*, from sinner to saved...

Megan Ross is from a small town in South Carolina, born and raised on cheese grits and tomato sandwiches. She is the wife to a loving husband with two beautiful daughters. When she isn't filling in as a dental hygienist, you can find her with family, teaching first-grade Sunday school or planning events with Faith and Family Fellowship ministries.

Note: First-time author Megan Ross gives an intimate testimony on how social media can affect one's mental health and how God intervened so she could have her redemption through Jesus Christ.

9 798893 455113